BULLYING

of related interest

Perspectives on Bullying
Ken Rigby
ISBN 1 85302 872 X

Stop the Bullying
A Handbook for Schools
Ken Rigby
ISBN 1 84310 070 3

Bullying in Schools
And What to Do About It
Ken Rigby
ISBN 1 85302 455 4

Troubles of Children and Adolescents
Edited by Ved Varma
ISBN 1 85302 323 X

The Anti-Bullying Game
Yvonne Searle and Isabelle Strong
ISBN 1 85302 335 3

BULLYING
A WHOLE-SCHOOL APPROACH

Amelia Suckling and Carla Temple

ILLUSTRATED BY

Christina Miesen

Jessica Kingsley Publishers
London and Philadelphia

First published in Australia by
Australian Council for Educational Research Limited

This edition published in the United Kingdom in 2002
by Jessica Kingsley Publishers Ltd
116 Pentonville Road
London N1 9JB, England
and
325 Chestnut Street
Philadelphia, PA 19106, USA

www.jkp.com

Copyright © 2001 Amelia Suckling and Carla Temple

Edited by Barbara Weiss
Text design by Captured Concepts
Illustrations by Christina Miesen

Library of Congress Cataloging in Publication Data
A CIP catalog record for this book is available from the Library of Congress

British Library Cataloguing in Publication Data
A CIP catalogue record for this book is available from the British Library

ISBN 1 84310 054 1

Printed and Bound in Great Britain by
Athenaeum Press, Gateshead, Tyne and Wear

Foreword

Before I could become a teacher, I was interviewed by a famous Professor of Education who asked 'What do you think is the most important quality a teacher can have?'. I replied, 'Empathy'. He thought for a while and said, 'I think, imagination'. That was over forty years ago and I have come to think we were both right. I am certain of it when I think about how schools need to respond to bullying: empathy, because we need to understand what it feels like to be bullied; imagination, because it's not enough simply to share another's sadness. We must also have ideas on how to help. These qualities, empathy with children and imagination, continually come through the work of the authors of this book. I am encouraged to think that their efforts will be rewarded.

Wisely, they build upon the work of others. They do not re-invent the wheel. There is now a body of sound and constructive advice on what schools and parents can do about bullying and this they communicate in a clear and interesting manner. But they go further than this. They address the question teachers now want to see answered: How, as classroom teachers, can we involve our students to work constructively with us in finding a solution to the vexed problem of bullying? I know that teachers feel they should be doing this and that they are often at a loss as to how to do it. This is where imagination comes in, and where we can learn a lot from Amelia Suckling and Carla Temple.

There are dozens of bright ideas in this book on how to work with children in classrooms. They are creative, practical and can be fun. Teachers will be grateful for the help they provide. Children will be happier in the knowledge that they understand themselves and others better, and are on the way to developing skills that will improve their relations with others. This without doubt is the best way to make bullying a thing of the past.

When I came to Australia in 1959 as a young teacher, the question of what qualities a teacher should have came up again. My new Principal, on the point of retirement, was prone to giving sage advice. The quality most needed, he said, was energy. Well, this is the third quality that these authors possess in abundance. I know that their seminar presentations are packed with energy. This book bears testimony to their sustained efforts in another way. In it they bring together an extensive body of knowledge about bullying in schools. And, what is more important, they provide practical answers to the perennial problem of how to stop the bullying.

Ken Rigby
Associate Professor, School of Education
University of South Australia

Acknowledgments

To bring this project to fruition would have been impossible without the support and enthusiasm of many generous people.

We wish to acknowledge the many primary-school teachers who, on completion of our teacher inservice sessions and student workshops, would ask, 'Have you got that in print?'. Their enthusiasm to address the bullying issue not only at a school level but also with their own students in class was a constant source of motivation.

We express gratitude to the many children who have shared with us their pain and feelings of frustration. Their brutal honesty and courage to relate these experiences has deepened our understanding of bullying and its many complexities. They have been a true source of inspiration.

Special thanks to Barbara Weiss, our editor, whose meticulous eye and genuine interest in the issue of bullying supported us in refining this book. Thanks to Pauline McClenahan for her skill in design and layout and to Christina Miesen, who has gracefully captured the thoughts and feelings of children through her illustrations.

We also wish to thank ACER for demonstrating, through the publication of this book, that bullying in schools is a serious issue that continually needs to be addressed.

Much gratitude and appreciation to our respective families and husbands Terry and Doug for being patient, understanding and for nurturing the family nest in the midst of work overload. To our collective four sons, Liam, Aymon, Max and Casey who, through their span of years – fourteen to five – have individually supported us in various ways, from speedy computer skills and the sharing of playground stories through to their kind words of love and encouragement.

Contents

Appendices

Introduction

There is no doubt that bullying in schools is insidious and difficult to manage and deal with — a complex issue that urgently demands effective action. We have found that bullying in the school environment can only be dealt with effectively if the whole school is behind the endeavour, that trying to handle it in isolation does not work in the long term.

We have a background in Special Education and share over forty years' teaching experience in primary schools and social adjustment centres. This has given us insight into and a realistic understanding of school culture. We now work as educational consultants, researching, developing and conducting a variety of teacher-training programs, parent sessions and personal development programs for children.

To deal with the covert nature of bullying we have developed a three-pronged approach that meets the needs of teachers, students and parents alike.

- We run inservice training for teachers that offers practical skills to identify quickly and deal with bullying behaviour and to handle parents' concerns when the subject of bullying is raised.
- We offer workshops for primary-school students that provide strategies for assertiveness when confronted with bullying and help them build resilience.
- Our parent information sessions help parents identify the possible signs of a bullied child, reinforce anti-bullying behaviour at home and help them to feel confident that the school is taking an active role in developing a strong anti-bullying policy.

Teachers in the majority of schools we visit are requesting assistance in dealing with the complex social issue of bullying. They want practical material that uses a multifaceted approach and is easy to implement.

We have thus felt compelled and inspired to write this book. Our primary focus is to show how crucial it is to involve the whole school community in creating and maintaining a school culture that values and practises an anti-bullying ethos. By adopting such a whole-school approach, members of the school community have the tools to create a dynamic, responsive and safe learning environment for all. Such an environment can make a significant and profound difference in students' lives.

How to use this book

We aim to present the material in a manner that is clear and gives up-to-date research and information, that will be of relevance to the teacher's particular situation and give practical intervention and prevention strategies and policy guidelines that are accessible and easy to use.

Part One is for all teachers in both primary and secondary schools. The key to success is for teachers to work collaboratively through this section, as it provides a solid foundation for implementing Part Two, which caters for students in middle- to upper-primary school. Part Two may well be taught within the health curriculum and presented sequentially or topics may be selected according to the needs of the students. The two sections can be used concurrently.

Part One: Building a Whole-school Approach explores ways in which teachers can collaborate with each other and other members of staff to formulate policy and practise building and maintaining a safe learning environment for the whole school community.

Part One offers:
- practical intervention and prevention strategies
- guidelines for formalising grievance procedures
- guidelines for developing and implementing an anti-bullying policy
- pro-forma documentation to assist with record-keeping
- ways of dealing with parents of the target and of the bully
- several checklists to assist with the development of a whole-school approach.

Part Two: Putting It Into Practice is geared specifically for students. It contains 15 lessons and each one includes:

Fact file, which gives brief, relevant background information for that lesson. It informs teachers of current issues. Reading the Fact File prior to the lesson may help the teacher structure the class so that all children feel comfortable to contribute in a meaningful way.

Purpose of lesson and *Learning outcomes*, which give the skills and understandings that students should gain on completing the lesson.

Materials required for that lesson – the ingredients.

Activities have been designed to encourage student participation at many levels. The activities invite students to:
- explore their values and attitudes regarding bullying behaviour
- identify and consider alternative behaviour to bullying and victim responses
- identify and consider the consequences of both bullying and victim behaviour
- develop communication skills.

What kids say will give teachers a realistic expectation of students' views on the topic.

Kids at work Each lesson has activities that the students complete on their own. This includes activity sheets (master copies are provided at the end of each lesson). These consolidate what has been learnt in the lesson.

Coaching tips provide helpful hints and reminders for the teacher.

Just for fun gives ideas for taking the concept further, if desired.

Appendix provides suppport material such as:
- a literature list for students
- sample letters to send to parents
- posters, which you may wish to enlarge
- an individual student management plan.

In general the term *victim* is not preferred unless citing a direct quote. Current terms being used for victim are *the target* and *the bullied*, which do not imply helplessness, hopelessness and permanency.

Teachers, of course, play a vital role in the success of a program such as is outlined in this book. Inevitably the message of building a safe and supportive learning environment for all is delivered to students both formally and informally through teachers' and the school's values, attitudes, beliefs and practices. Students are most attentive to the hidden curriculum – how teachers speak to students, colleagues, parents: how they choose to handle negative and confronting behaviour in the classroom and the playground; how well they listen to, follow up and follow through on their students' fears and concerns; and how and what they teach.

Aims

Our overall aims can be put quite simply. We want to foster a committed social responsibility within the school community so that effective changes can occur, using a whole-school approach.

We aim to empower students and teachers with appropriate strategies that will enable them to build a safe and supportive learning environment for all.

We provide strategies and tools that aim to develop resilience in students so that conflict can build character rather than destroy it.

And last but certainly not least, we aim to nurture in students a sense of empathy for the target when witnessing a bullying incident and an ability to follow through with safe and sensible bystander actions.

Learning outcomes

From our experience we see the following outcomes and *actions* as a vital and inevitable part of a safe school environment.

Students will be able to:
- *engage* in responsible reporting when witnessing or experiencing injustice
- *identify* bullying behaviour
- *demonstrate* a repertoire of self-management strategies
- *build* resilience so as to free oneself of thinking like a victim
- *feel* empathy for targeted members of the school community and, as a result, take safe and sensible action as a bystander.

Teachers will be able to:
- *acknowledge* that reducing bullying is a shared responsibility within and across the school
- *implement* prevention and intervention strategies that involve the whole school through exploring possibilities and solutions in collaboration with others across the broad spectrum of the school community
- *empower* students to deal with conflict in constructive ways
- *create* opportunities for students to develop a social conscience (formally and informally) and to be able to act on this as the occasion arises.

Expectations

As a dedicated team committed to anti-bullying in the school, teachers' expectations can realistically be:
- an increase in bystanders that are pro-active
- an increase in the number of students feeling comfortable and safe to tell an adult about a bullying incident
- a large percentage of students believing their school actively takes a stand against bullying

- a decrease in the number of students being bullied
- an increase in staff morale due to consistency throughout the school in following through on policy and procedures that have been established.

When working with students, we operate from the premise that there are no right or wrong answers, only many possibilities and solutions in creating and building a safe school for everyone.

We wish you and your school community the best of luck as you journey together, exploring values, beliefs, attitudes and practices regarding bullying. We hope that many, many possibilities and solutions are voiced and transformed into shared best practice.

PART ONE

DEVELOPING A WHOLE-SCHOOL APPROACH

CHAPTER 1

The importance of a
whole-school approach

This book is based on the belief that schools need to adopt a whole-school approach for effecting a long-term and positive influence on their school environment. This is particularly important when creating and maintaining a school culture that values and practises an anti-bullying ethos.

The avenues for changing to and maintaining an inclusive, safe and supportive school culture are many and varied. A whole-school approach tackles bullying from as many angles and across as broad a spectrum of the school community as possible. It addresses bullying at the levels of prevention and intervention. It takes into account:

- the style and quality of leadership and management practices
- the quality and delivery of curriculum
- playground activities and the quality of supervision
- the formalised and agreed procedures to deal with a bullying incident
- building relationships with others and with self.

The whole-school approach is based on shared values, beliefs and attitudes within the school community.

Schools are acknowledging that individual approaches, whereby the teacher acts in isolation to resolve bullying and its ramifications, are short-sighted and ineffectual for the entire school community.

We hope that Diagram 1 on page 8 and the following rationale illustrate the importance of adopting a whole-school approach. We believe that school culture is influenced when the school community (teachers, administrators, students and parents) can articulate their shared values and translate these into a dynamic and responsive policy and practice.

Diagram 1 illustrates the importance of acknowledging and developing the interdependence of the whole school and the individual. When these elements are in balance and a shared vision has been articulated, the school ethos can be transformed.

Rationale

The rationale underlying this book is complex and involves many aspects; these are explored on the following pages. One factor they all share, however, is the need to adopt a whole-school approach and to present questions for teachers and educators so that they can review their current school practice and its underlying beliefs.

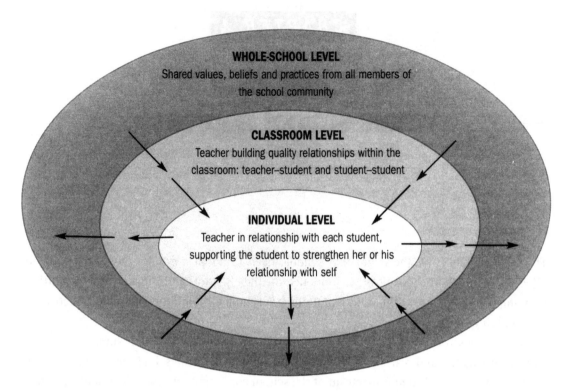

WHOLE-SCHOOL LEVEL
Shared values, beliefs and practices from all members of the school community

CLASSROOM LEVEL
Teacher building quality relationships within the classroom: teacher–student and student–student

INDIVIDUAL LEVEL
Teacher in relationship with each student, supporting the student to strengthen her or his relationship with self

Diagram 1 Illustrating the interdependence between the individual and the whole school.

Social context

Bullying is regarded as violence, whether it is physical, verbal, blatant or subtle. In our modern society violence is growing in our homes, in public places and in what we see through the media. Our values can be influenced by these social changes: children become desensitised to violence and violence becomes the norm, for many a means to an end. Many families are exposed to crime, domestic violence and media overload and often feel unsupported as they witness the deterioration of social systems (neighbourhoods, extended families, communities and religious practices), which once supported them and are now slowly disappearing.

There is thus a growing pressure on schools to provide the stable structure that will foster community values such as co-operation and responsibility, values that our society so very much needs.

Unfortunately many people in our community have ideas and attitudes to bullying that are complacent and unsupportive. Some believe that it is a normal part of growing up and even character building. Fortunately, in recent years bullying has been considered an important social problem that requires attention. For children and adolescents it is their biggest fear. Galton and Wilcocks say that 'children put bullying at the top of their list of fears; indeed children may be more afraid of other children than the deviant adults we so often warn them about' (cited in Besag, 1989, p. 111).

Others in the community are quick to blame the school when bullying arises. According to the work of Peter Randall (1996, p. 2), 'schools do not create bullying; at best they merely import it from the communities they serve, at worst they allow it to flourish by not giving it the constant attention it deserves'.

There can be no doubt that where schools conscientiously and vigorously implement an anti-bullying policy, an environment of fairness and safety is achievable. When schools fail to implement such policy and allow bullying, they impede maturity by denying students the opportunity to develop normally through social interaction.

As schools, do we have the support systems in place to address violence and thus fill the void that is so sadly lacking in society?

Community expectations

The community has certain expectations and beliefs about schools providing a duty of care which makes them legally responsible for the educational development of students while in the school environment. 'Schools are responsible for providing safe and supportive learning environments where all students can participate equally without discrimination and fear' (House of Representatives Standing Committee on Employment, Education and Training, 1993).

As teachers, are we informed with up-to-date practices and do we have the skills to create a safe learning environment for all students?

The damaging effects of bullying

Much worldwide research has been done into the damaging effects of bullying. Olweus (1993) found that teenage boys who became victims between the ages of 13 and 16 were more likely to suffer depression and have low self-esteem by the age of 23 (cited in Randall, 1996). Research by Sharp and Thompson, which involved approximately 700 secondary-school students, indicated that of the students bullied, one-fifth said they would truant from school in order to avoid the bullying, one-third experienced difficulty focusing on their school work and approximately one-fifth felt physically ill after experiencing bullying (cited in Randall, 1996).

What is more alarming are the disturbing long-term consequences. Gilmartin (1987) found that in later life children who had been bullied experienced difficulty developing close and intimate relationships based on trust. In longitudinal studies (Farrington, 1993) it was found that children who were bullied at school were more likely to parent children who exhibited victim behaviour, hence the cycle continues.

Bullying not only has devastating effects for the target but also for the bully. A Norwegian study followed thousands of boys from the early years at school through to their adult life and found that as high as 65 per cent of those identified as bullies had criminal convictions by the age of 24 (Olweus, 1993).

As teachers, do we have in place effective strategies that will support students who are on a downward spiral and help them to build resilience?

Schools as social environments

Current thinking in the community assumes that the target of the bullying and/or the bully are having difficulties emotionally and socially, which determines their behaviour. The solution is to lay blame and punish. With such thinking, bully/target problems are handled using only an 'individual approach' and such approaches are usually short-term and ineffective.

Bullying often occurs as a result of the social environment, not simply the psychology of the individual bully. Sharp and Smith (1994a) support this by saying that bullying is found in group settings. Its solution requires collective responsibility.

If patterns of bullying are not challenged they can become ingrained in the school culture and self-perpetuating (Nottingshire Education Committee, ch. 11 in Smith & Thompson, 1991). If teachers fail to take action they may be considered as colluders, contributing to an unsafe learning environment for their students.

As teachers, can we move beyond an approach that focuses on the individual problem to implementing both prevention and intervention strategies that will positively influence the entire school community and help build a safe and supportive learning environment for all school members?

Impact of the teacher

Teachers have a significant impact on students and contribute enormously to building student well-being and effective learning through who they are as individuals and what and how they teach.

Many students do not have the opportunity to experience a 'significant other', other than in the school environment. Teachers therefore become the only effective channel for change; the parents/family may feel ill-equipped to handle problems constructively or may have contributed to the problem.

As teachers, do we have the skills and strategies to maximise each student's learning experiences?

Breaking the cycle

It is unfortunate that in many cases there is only motivation for change at times of crisis. Teachers need to break the cycle by implementing strategies for prevention so that if a bullying incident does develop, students and staff are equipped to manage it.

Can personal skills be taught as a regular component of curriculum rather than being born out of crisis? If students are provided with a repertoire of self-management strategies built on the development of social conscience, the victim cycle can be broken but, more importantly, need not be experienced.

As teachers, can we provide our students with a repertoire of skills so that they can go about the business of changing their state of mind? a state of mind where each student develops a sense of self-worth, hope, persistence, optimism and resilience?

It was through our conversations with teachers and observing the challenging questions they must face on a daily basis that we came to write this book, and to address the issue of reducing bullying by focusing on the values, attitudes and beliefs within and throughout the community.

A working model for a whole-school approach is shown in Diagram 2. Each of its four components is elaborated on in Chapters 3, 4, 5 and 6. The strategies offered in these chapters may assist you and your colleagues to evaluate current policy and practices and affirm the positive actions your school may have already implemented.

CURRICULUM

1 Interpersonal skills
2 Teaching/learning styles
3 Curriculum content
   - literature
   - videos
   - drama
   - debates
   - music
   - guest speakers
   - social skills programs
4 Extra-curricular programs for selected students

PLAYGROUND SUPERVISION

1 Suitable activities for wet-day timetable
2 Lunchtime interest groups
3 Plan and layout of playgrounds and buildings
4 Extra staff when needed
5 Availability of sports equipment
6 Split lunchtimes and shortened recess, lunchtime
7 Spot-check trouble spots
8 Remind vulnerable children where to play
9 Staff briefing
10 Three-tier lunchtime

PREVENTION AND INTERVENTION

SCHOOL STRUCTURE

1 Classroom meeting
2 Quality Circles
3 Buddy system
4 Welcoming Committee
5 Peer mediation
6 Student Representative Council
7 Transition programs
8 Home–school liaison
9 Status and time given to the Student Welfare Co-ordinator
10 Regular school assemblies that support, inform and promote positive school ethos
11 Relevant student management policy and anti-bullying policy
12 Structures that invite family involvement
13 Safety House
14 Community network

DEALING WITH A BULLYING INCIDENT

Non-punitive Approach
Method of Shared Concern
No Blame Approach

Punitive Approach
Clearly identified rules with logical consequences
Time-out
Denial of privileges with a way back
Individual student management plan
Suspension
Expulsion

Diagram 2 Model for a whole-school approach to bullying.

CHAPTER 2

Curriculum

'Curriculum refers to all the experiences through which knowledge, skills and values are communicated at school. It encompasses formally planned curriculum content, informal or unplanned curriculum content, informal or unplanned messages and the ways in which this information is structured and communicated.' (Education Department of Queensland, 1998, p. 17)

Curriculum is no longer about passing on facts and information. It is a powerful means for affecting the beliefs, values and attitudes of students.

With these definitions in mind a teacher may well question:

- what to teach
- how to teach it
- why teach it.

It is imperative that teachers' practices and methodologies are broad and support students' learning styles.

Curriculum thus consists of many layers. The curriculum *content* (subjects/timetables) is the most obvious and often what is seen first, but underpinning it is the hidden curriculum.

CONTENT/SUBJECTS

SOCIAL SKILLS	DRAMA
LITERATURE	MUSIC
DEBATING	ART

TEACHING/LEARNING STYLES

Inclusive	Equitable
Celebrates cultural diversity	Student-centred learning
Culturally appropriate	Emphasis on personal best
Co-operative groupings	Team building
Challenges stereotypes	

INTERPERSONAL SKILLS

Building quality relationships within the school community

student–student　　teacher–student　　teacher–parent　　teacher–teacher　　student with self

Teachers as role models promoting a shared understanding of respect and fairness.

Diagram 3 The curriculum – an overview.

The hidden curriculum includes *teaching/learning styles* — how the class is organised and the teacher's approach to the learning situation — and the *interpersonal skills* the teacher models to students. Diagram 3 illustrates the layers contained in the curriculum.

Exploring the Curriculum Model

Interpersonal skills

The foundation on which the curriculum is built is the interpersonal skills of the teacher and how he or she can form quality relationships within the school community.

Teachers can play a crucial role in changing students' behaviour. They are influential in helping students to relate to others in their peer group and to form ideas and beliefs about who and what they are.

Teachers are powerful role models for their students and are in the ideal situation to encourage healthy social development and positive relationships within the school community.

This can be a daunting responsibility: teachers' attitudes, values and beliefs are reflected through their behaviour and this in turn is interpreted by their students. It is not surprising how astute students are in recognising this hidden curriculum, observing the teacher's body language, tone of voice and use of spoken language and how this influences their learning and relationships. Students very readily pick up the unspoken messages that people convey through body language and individual ways of being and operating.

As mentioned on page 10, a teacher may be the only effective role model some students have, a model who can possibly inspire and be a channel for change. The benefits of positive relationship building have long been recognised. It is common knowledge that positive relationships encourage self-esteem and self-confidence, which in turn facilitate one's ability to alter circumstances for the better.

Teaching/learning styles

When using curriculum as a tool for building a supportive school culture, consider the following:

- Approaches are sequential and progressive throughout the school.
- Approaches implemented are age, gender and culturally appropriate and relevant.
- The message is consistent across the school curriculum.
- Approaches address the values, attitudes and behaviour of the students, parents and teachers within a social context.

Students usually have a preferred learning style or mode in which they absorb information/concepts and so on more readily. These are the kinesthetic, auditory and visual modes. Below we give each learning style followed by a list of tasks that are particularly appropriate for that way of learning.

Kinesthetic learners

These learn best through:

- doing
- team games
- role-plays
- coaching other students
- demonstrating to the class
- making models
- attending excursions
- writing on butcher paper, mini-chalkboards and whiteboards
- evoking strong emotional images (that they can get into!)
- hands-on experiences
- experiments
- touching, feeling.

These students learn best when they can do.

Visual learners

These learn best through:

- cartoons
- flashcards
- use of colours
- variety of shapes, sizes
- shades of brightness
- visual displays
- posters, charts
- graphs
- slogans
- mind maps
- videos
- slides
- film
- books
- an overview (see the big picture in their mind)
- photographs
- maps and plans
- creative visualisation.

These students learn best when they can access visuals.

Auditory learners

These learn best through:

- debates
- jokes
- music
- buzz pairs
- discussions

- listening to guest speakers
- speeches
- audio tapes
- stories read to them
- coming up with slogans
- using mnemonics
- playing with words, sounds and phrases
- listening games
- variety in rate of speech, tone, volume and pitch
- making up scripts for role-plays.

These students learn best when they can use their hearing as a primary focus.

Curriculum content

Tackling bullying through the curriculum provides students with a systematic approach. When teachers deal with the issue using a variety of teaching/learning styles, students can begin to examine, investigate and understand their own attitude and behaviour towards bullying. This process invites students to develop, practise and implement their own solutions to the problem and take responsibility for these.

Teachers should keep in mind that no matter how sophisticated the curriculum, what teaching styles or learning techniques are used, the underlying and most important factor in the successful education of a child is the respect he or she is given.

Literature

For some students literature may serve as a catalyst for change. They may experience a sense of relief when the characters of a book portray the same feelings of loneliness, emotional pain and shame experienced through being bullied. The burden and isolation of the feeling and thought that says 'I'm the only one that ever gets bullied' can begin to be unravelled and explored at a safe distance.

Needless to say, the literature will need to be age and issue related. Books will vary from picture books through to older fiction. Poems, rhymes, riddles and chants can also be explored. See the Appendices, page 142, for a list of suitable books.

Videos

Many students are exposed to violence, oppression and discrimination through videos and television programs. By the time adolescents have left high school, they will have experienced approximately 15 000 hours of television compared with 11 000 hours spent at school. During that time they would have witnessed some 18 000 violent acts, such as murder, arson and robbery (Oskamp, 1984). The glorification of violence has desensitised children. Thoughtful selection of videos by the teacher can help re-educate children's feelings.

Drama

'Drama can help extend and deepen the students' understanding of peer conflict. It can also help establish that bullying behaviour is to a certain extent a matter of choice and responsibility' (Gobey, ch. 7, p. 71, in Smith & Thompson, 1991). Drama is a positive way of approaching the problem from the perspectives of the bullied, the bully and the bystander.

If students are working in an environment that is active, invites participation and co-operation, drama works as a positive tool that is both fun and adventurous. Drama provides a place for trial and error and experimentation with stereotypes. It teaches students that negotiation, problem-solving and co-operation are elements of a challenging and gradual process.

Debates

Debates are suitable for students in upper primary school. They give the students opportunity to articulate for their peers in a systematic manner the many angles from which bullying can be viewed. Ask students for possible debating topics. Prior to the debate students will need to collect data. The debates could be presented at school assembly if students feel comfortable with this.

Music

Music is an excellent tool for engaging feelings. Students could write and produce a jingle or slogan for a television or radio commercial that depicts the school's stand on bullying. Alternatively, using a less direct approach, the teacher could invite students to listen (and draw) to a selection of musical pieces that arouse feelings of joy, fear, oppression, power, violence, harmony and so on. Use this to stimulate discussion.

Guest speakers

Well-selected and appropriate guest speakers can enhance the curriculum by providing another perspective on bullying, giving the topic further depth, meaning and relevance for students. The guest speakers should support the values, beliefs and attitudes of the school community. Guest speakers can range from theatre/drama groups, speakers on social issues, to local police, students from visiting schools and sportsmen and women.

Social skills

It would be wrong to assume that social skills are innate. It is important that these are taught as they effect how children approach school and family life.

Creating a safe and comfortable environment is crucial for the success of teaching social skills. The teacher must bring a genuine interest and desire to build quality relationships. He or she must also offer flexible and creative teaching/learning styles to nurture students in the acquisition and maintenance of new skills. This demands well-developed interpersonal skills and broad, engaging practices aligned with the ethos of the school.

It is important to keep in mind that the development of social skills is a significant part of school life and prevails across the entire curriculum and school community. It is reflected in the attitudes, values, beliefs and behaviour of that community and is not just a curriculum component timetabled for a set day in a set place.

As with academic learning, students develop social skills at different levels and speeds. Some students present in the classroom and playground with excellent social skills, others present with none. Some students will require much assistance in the acquisition of new skills. These skills may need to be broken down into specific segments and practised many times in order to be understood. No doubt these skills will be challenged regularly, particularly when real-life issues arise within the classroom or playground; students can then put into place what they have learned in a meaningful and realistic way. Many children may require a cue or prompt to assist them in their new skill. Teachers could prompt with the question: 'Is there another way we could solve this?'.

Skills to focus on may include:

- dealing with conflict
- assertiveness training
- making and maintaining friendships
- co-operation
- developing empathy through being aware of one's feelings and the feelings of others
- problem-solving
- standing up for oneself without being aggressive or manipulative
- coping strategies such as relaxation, self-talk and creative visualisation.

Argyle (1983) believes that the components of social skills include:

- reading a situation and the intentions of others in that situation
- developing a plan on how best to respond
- implementing the plan and noting its effects on others
- modifying this when necessary.

The process as outlined above requires careful planning, modelling and rehearsing.

Sessions are best run in a mixed group with an awareness and sensitivity about grouping students appropriately, where all students feel comfortable to participate and contribute.

Social skills can be taught in a variety of ways, depending on the teacher's individual style and the nature of the group (refer to teaching/learning styles, pages 13–15 to assist planning). Some of these ways are listed below.

- The teacher models specific behaviours, making the distinction between reacting and staying in control.
- The teacher gives students opportunities to rehearse the new behaviour/skill as many times as is necessary.
- The teacher provides script cards that are easy for students to read and relevant to their experiences.
- Puppets or masks can be used by students who feel self-conscious.
- When working with the entire class the teacher asks the students to make a circle and turn their backs into the centre of the circle. In this way the students do not have to be facing anyone. The particular skill can be rehearsed as a group, then when confidence and comfort levels have increased the teacher asks the students to face back into the centre of the circle.
- No student should be made to feel threatened by rehearsing the skill in front of the class when they are not yet ready. Perhaps the student can be taken aside to practise alone with the teacher and/or a friend if necessary.

Extra-curricular programs for selected students

If the school believes that a support group is necessary for specific students who have experienced *long-term* difficulties with bullying, it is important to keep some issues in mind, such as:

- how will the sessions take place?
- what will the sessions be called?
- how will other students perceive the sessions?

Without consideration of the above issues the school may create the situation that serves to enhance the self-fulfilling prophecy of students labelled as either bullies or victims. Discretion is of prime importance.

The aim of a support group for bullied students should be to change the status of the students. The key skills to be taught are handling bullying behaviour and avoiding bullying. In such a group students can seek support, make friendships and rehearse strategies in a safe, small and caring environment. The group should be kept small (six to eight students), facilitated by a trained and sensitive leader (who will not advertise the inadequacies of the group), and run on a voluntary basis. Parents should be informed so that students can rehearse their repertoire of new skills at home with parental support. The teacher may run these sessions for approximately six weeks.

When working with students who have experienced long-term bullying, it is imperative that teachers and administrators first question:
- leadership practices
- management practices
- level of supervision
- grievance procedures
- intervention and prevention strategies
- level of outside professional help accessed
- current anti-bullying policy.

Summary

Curriculum can be a dynamic and responsive tool for building a safe, inclusive and supportive learning environment for the school community. Underpinning the success of curriculum as an influential and effective tool are the following:
- acknowledging the existence of a hidden curriculum
- building quality relationships within the school community
- providing role models that promote a shared understanding of respect, fairness and responsibility
- implementing inclusive teaching practices
- adopting approaches that address the values, attitudes and behaviour of the individual and the school community
- creating opportunities for students to develop and act upon a social conscience.

Such values and practices build an infrastructure that disadvantages bullying throughout the whole school.

CHECKLIST

Curriculum considerations

The curriculum (content, teaching/learning styles and interpersonal skills) is a tool for effecting change in students and in the school community. This checklist has been devised to assist in planning curriculum so that it caters for individual students and build a supportive school culture.

Interpersonal skills

Do I:

☐ use respectful language when speaking to parents, students and colleagues?

☐ encourage students positively to deal with relationship issues?

☐ set high standards of courtesy and citizenship?

☐ model appropriate behaviour to students, parents and colleagues?

☐ nurture and encourage students to explore new friendships?

☐ develop and maintain a climate of respect?

☐ implement a repertoire of student management strategies that allows students to self-correct and develop self-control?

Teaching/learning styles

Does my teaching practice reflect:

☐ an inclusive classroom (catering for individual differences)?

☐ an equitable classroom?

☐ an emphasis on personal best?

☐ a non-competitive tone through using co-operative group activities?

☐ a respect for students' cultural diversity?

☐ time given for free exploration?

☐ student-centred learning?

Content

Is the curriculum content broad, encompassing skill development in the areas of:

☐ English?

☐ mathematics?

☐ science?

☐ technology?

☐ studies of society and environment?

☐ health and physical education?

☐ languages other than English?

☐ the arts?

CHAPTER 3

School structure

Johnson and Johnson (1994) illustrate clearly the importance of school structure by stating that behaviour is 85 per cent determined by organisational structure and the individual determines the remaining 15 per cent. Schools therefore have an enormous responsibility in creating organisational and leadership practices that support all students.

The structure in schools has changed considerably over the years with the expectation that teachers are to meet the many needs of students – emotionally, academically and socially. Schools obviously can no longer focus on the 3Rs alone.

Teachers constantly share with us how overloaded they are with having to wear so many hats in meeting the pressing needs of their students and their students' parents. There are expectations to be nurse, police officer and marriage counsellor with more and more emphasis on welfare; this can be overwhelming. Therefore, do schools have organisational and leadership practices that can sustain and strengthen teachers when addressing the complex needs that arise in a school community? Below are examples of practices where teachers can support their students and their students' parents, and students can support their peers.

Classroom meetings

Classroom meetings provide a forum for students to discuss many issues, one of which may be bullying. These meetings give students the opportunity to raise issues, and be involved in the processes of problem-solving and decision-making that will affect both themselves and fellow class members.

Running a classroom meeting requires planning. Some issues to consider prior to conducting a meeting with your class are listed below.

- Re-arrange classroom seating. A change of space can bring about a change in thinking. Some teachers have students arrange their chairs in a semi-circle or circle. This seating arrangement allows for all children to be seen and heard.
- A meeting lasts for 20–30 minutes: any longer and the students' attention span diminishes.
- Create a non-threatening tone in the classroom whereby all students feel comfortable to contribute.
- Keep the meeting specific. You may wish to use an agenda that is either written on the board or a handout.
- Develop rules for the class meeting, for example: look and listen; respect others' ideas; what is said in the meeting is only for the class.
- Steer students towards solution-focused thinking. Do the solutions focus on respect, and are they relevant and reasonable?

- To avoid the situation of particular children dominating the meeting and the same child never contributing, give each student three to five counters each. With each contribution a counter is used. This gives the teacher quick and visual feedback (Rogers, 1994).

Quality Circles

A Quality Circle (Cowie & Sharp, ch. 4, in Sharp & Smith, 1994a) consists of five to twelve people. Its task is to identify ways of improving the school's organisation. Quality Circles can be used as a forum in which students can discuss and deal with the issue of bullying. This strategy is suitable for students in upper primary and secondary schools.

Quality Circles are best run on a weekly basis for approximately 45 minutes. In dealing with and solving a problem, the Quality Circle moves through five distinct steps:

1 determining the problem
2 brainstorming possible causes
3 finding a solution to the problem
4 offering solutions to senior teachers for feedback
5 reviewing and evaluating the solutions offered.

1 Determining the problem

Students brainstorm features of school life that are problematic. These are listed on a large sheet of butcher paper (by scribe). There is no discussion at this stage. Students take turns to share ideas around the circle. If a student does not have anything to contribute, he or she can 'pass'. Items listed are prioritised (through voting procedure).

2 Brainstorming possible causes

Here the Quality Circle looks for possible causes of the problem, breaking it down into a series of *why* questions (see Diagram 4).

As well as using this technique, students may wish to look for possible causes by collecting data and:

- interviewing a sample of students
- making observations during an agreed time slot
- conducting a survey.

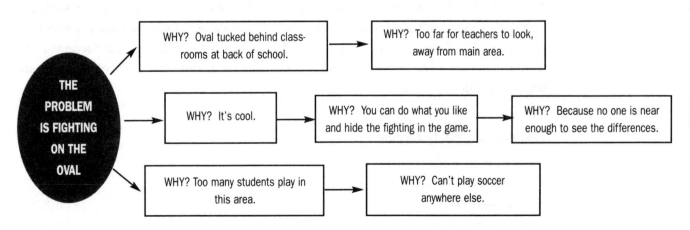

Diagram 4 Using the Why? Why? technique.

3   Developing a solution

When the members of the Quality Circle have identified the problem, possible solutions can then be explored. At this stage a series of *how* questions are asked (the How? How? technique, Diagram 5) so that an action plan can be formulated. Members of the group take on three defined roles to assist in this process. The inquirer's role is to ask 'how?' until all possibilities are exhausted. The respondent's role is to answer these questions and the observer's role is to record the answers that are given. When all the *how* questions have been answered, the Quality Circle members then discuss the advantages and disadvantages of the proposals offered and how costly and realistic the solutions are.

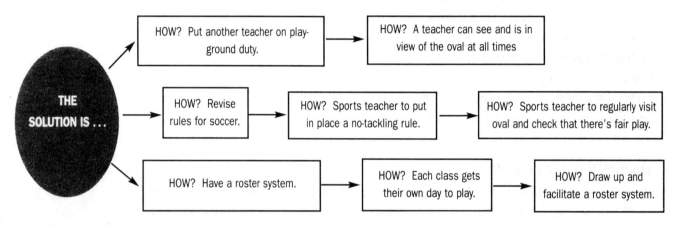

Diagram 5   Using the How? How? technique.

4   Offering a solution

Members of the Quality Circle prepare a presentation, outlining the solutions they have explored. The principal and senior teachers are the ones to approach as they are the decision-makers. Encourage the students to prepare a professional presentation using a variety of presentation techniques. They must have a thorough knowledge concerning the problem and its possible solutions and be confident to handle queries and questions that may arise.

5   Reviewing and evaluating the solution

The team of senior teachers and/or principal will decide on the suitability of the students' proposed solutions. If the team decides not to carry out the solutions, the matter is discussed with the Quality Circle members to establish why. If the proposed solutions are accepted, the team of senior teachers will implement and evaluate these and then feedback to the members of the Quality Circle.

Benefits of Quality Circles

Quality Circles teach students to:
- co-operate with their peers
- listen to others
- share their ideas
- prioritise, record and analyse

- formulate solutions
- evaluate solutions
- present solutions.

Roles for students

Victimised students often feel more comfortable talking about their bullying experiences with their peers. Studies undertaken by Rigby (1996) and Slee indicate that if a student is to tell at all, they will first tell a friend, followed by their mother, then their father and last of all, a teacher.

The school may wish to select a core of interested students who exhibit the social skills required to support students who are having difficulties socially and to welcome new students. These selected students are trained and given an appropriate role description so that they can effectively make a caring contribution to the school. The roles include: being a buddy, a member of a Welcoming Committee, a peer mediator or being part of the Junior Council.

Buddy system

The buddy system, in which one student supports and looks out for the other, can be enormously beneficial in situations involving bullying. Careful selection of the buddy by the teacher is of prime importance. However, no student should be made to feel that they 'have to' be a buddy. The teacher may select an older student or a student from the same class. The buddy can be both observer and companion. The bullied student would benefit if the buddy had similar interests and was someone with kudos among his or her peers.

The advantages for the bullied of having a buddy are that it provides:

- protection
- a model of assertive behaviour
- a model of social behaviour such as joining and participating in groups
- increased self-esteem
- the experience of friendship.

See Lesson 9, 'Buddies', on pages 107–9 for further discussion and activities on the topic.

Welcoming Committee

This idea developed when a group of teachers were sharing with us their concerns and frustrations regarding the exclusion of a new Year 5 girl from Ireland. The Welcoming Committee exists as a preventative measure which schools can easily adopt. There could be three Welcoming Committees in a school, comprising respectively junior, middle and senior students, depending on the size of the school. Students are selected for their ability to 'make others feel comfortable', that is students with well-developed social skills. The students selected may develop a list of tasks appropriate to the occasion and ascribe one or more to each committee member. Here is a sample:

- show new student around the school
- bring a game to share
- invite him or her to join your games
- ring the student at home to check on how the day went

- arrange to meet the student in the morning where he or she is dropped off (this can often be an anxious time for new and/or bullied students)
- bring some playlunch to share.

You will find that students express creative and practical ideas when given the opportunity.

Peer mediation

Peer mediation is a means of handling conflict in a pro-active way without directly or always involving an adult. It can be a tool that supports and complements the school's student management policy.

Peer mediation is a process where students (volunteered, selected and trained) mediate disputes among their peers. These are usually minor disputes; students should never be put in a position of handling serious peer conflict. The mediators work in pairs to help their peers resolve disputes.

Their role is to help the parties involved understand the problem from each side and assist them in reaching an agreed solution. The mediators are trained not to impose their own solutions but to steer the disputants towards an agreed solution. The students who are trained abide by four rules:

1 don't interrupt
2 no put-downs or name-calling
3 be as honest as you can
4 agree to solve the problem.

Peer mediation can occur in the playground or a mediation room. Peer mediators usually wear something that makes them identifiable in the playground. Some schools use badges, differently coloured hats and/or set up a reporting table with umbrellas in the playground.

Each school will need to make decisions on a variety of issues relating to mediation, such as:

- how will peer mediators be selected?
- how will they be identified by other students?
- where will they mediate?
- on which disputes will they mediate?

Adopting peer mediation has many benefits for teachers, students and parents. Such benefits are:

- teachers spend less time on handling disputes
- the skill of mediation is a valuable life skill
- it improves the tone within the school
- it gives students another avenue to voice their concerns and devise solutions.

For any strategy to be successful within school time, effort and commitment are necessary. Peer mediators need to be well selected, trained and supported.

Some parents and teachers may initially resist peer mediation, believing that it wastes too much time that the student does not have and/or that students will be mediating on issues that adults should handle. When presenting peer mediation as a strategy, the following need to be considered:

- teachers' and parents' fears and concerns
- who constitutes the leadership team that supports the peer mediators
- how to implement the strategy

- benefits of adopting this strategy
- what are the short-term and long-term goals.

Student Representative Council / Junior Council

The Student Representative Council, if given guidelines, support and encouragement, can play an influential and dynamic role in the school. It can voice students' concerns on a variety of issues and formulate possible solutions. If well steered, the Student Representative Council can raise the awareness of school bullying, develop strategies and publicise these. It may become a comfortable forum for students to discuss bullying, and create a process of change in students' values, attitudes and beliefs on the issue.

Transition programs

Transition programs operating from pre-school to school, from primary to secondary school or for new students moving into the school at any level help ensure adequate integration and hence reduce the students' fears. Many schools are now doing great work in this area so that new students can settle in with ease. Support through effective transition programs help prevent the development of delinquency and substance abuse (Felner & Adan, 1988).

Home–school liaison

Research indicates that the level of bullying seems inversely correlated to the degree that staff are involved in the lives of their students. Some students require more input than others. Building a link with the student's home in a professional capacity can provide enormous support for both student and family.

The home–school liaison in the form of face-to-face chats between the teacher and parent is particularly important for some students, either at school or at the student's home. More informal ways of communicating can be provided through:

- notes from the teacher
- phone calls
- communication diary
- student diary
- school newsletters.

The Student Welfare Co-ordinator

Working towards solutions in dealing with bullying requires enormous time and energy, which often falls on the shoulders of the Student Welfare Co-ordinator. Time is required to do the 'homework' around the incident, speaking with the bystanders, target and bullies, providing follow-up to review solutions and strategies and, where necessary, communicating with parents and relevant teachers. This is many hours of work. The Student Welfare Co-ordinator needs to be allocated sufficient time, support and have positive status in the school that is recognised by all students. Also, if students notice that senior members of staff are giving up their time to be involved, it is seen as serious in their eyes.

School assemblies

Regular school assemblies that support, inform and promote the school ethos can serve as an excellent vehicle for reinforcing anti-bullying. Assemblies need to be kept brief and engage all students. Assemblies may be conducted by students, and hosted and organised by different classes. It can be a time to acknowledge the skills, strengths and citizenship of students. It can become a structure that sends the message: 'our school is a safe and happy place'.

Student management policy

There are many names given for student management policy. Some schools use the term student welfare policy, pastoral care policy, discipline policy or behaviour management policy. Regardless of the name used and the model adopted, the policy needs to be preventative, corrective and supportive of teachers and students. Rogers (1998) defines these as follows:

preventative: being concerned with the basic rights of students, with clear rules and consequences, contracting with students, and the running of the classroom in an equitable manner.

corrective: teachers correct disruptive, anti-social or disruptive behaviour.

supportive: ensuring correction is carried out in a fair manner and that the teacher re-establishes a positive relationship with the disciplined student.

The goal behind such a policy is to create a fair and consistent approach that will help establish a safe and positive school environment: an environment where students can learn and teachers can teach. Such a policy develops:
- self-control in students
- responsibility for behaviour and the opportunity to experience the consequences of one's choices
- students' abilities to recognise the rights, responsibilities of themselves and others
- positive social behaviour towards self and community.

When teachers adopt an assertive, positive and consistent approach and follow up and follow through on issues of student behaviour based on agreed and well-publicised practices, the likelihood of students feeling confused, angry and hostile is reduced.

Some schools have their anti-bullying policy as part of their student management policy or as a well-defined policy. Regardless of this, the content needs to be relevant, implementation needs to be thorough, and the policy needs to be reviewed and evaluated regularly. (Guidelines for developing an anti-bullying policy are given in Chapter 6, pages 48–57.)

Family involvement

Many parents wish to take the opportunity to be involved in their child's school life but may not know how to or what is available. If schools can provide a variety of opportunities (well advertised) that invite family involvement, the link between school and home becomes stronger. Below are ways that will encourage parental involvement.

- Invite parents to formal and informal school functions.
- Offer courses relevant to the needs of the parent group.
- Invite parents to assist on excursions.
- Have a parent-to-parent buddy system.
- Employ a parent liaison officer.
- Invite parents to assist with specific programs in the classroom.
- Make parents aware of who they need to contact if their child is experiencing problems.

Safety House

An adult member of the community offers their home as protection for children who may feel unsafe on their journey to and from school. Children are able to identify easily a Safety House in their area by its familiar logo. A Safety House helps link the school and the wider community. As teachers, we need to make our students aware of what a Safety House means, how to recognise it and where it is located in the community.

Some teachers take their students for a neighbourhood walk, locating a Safety House close to the school. Perhaps invite your Safety House representative to meet your students so that they can recognise who he or she is if the need should arise; inform your students of the representative's role in the community. This helps to build community spirit and demonstrates the value of partnership.

Building a network

Schools need to be aware of the resources available in the community and within the school system and develop a relationship with these organisations. They also need to be aware of the cultural, ethnic and religious backgrounds of the families in their school community. This will enable them to refer the students and families to the appropriate resources. Schools can then better serve the needs of their students, the parents and staff.

The network may include government departments and services, private organisations, individuals and community-based non-government organisations. To ensure efficiency and effectiveness the school needs to put in place a clear referral procedure with a good understanding of the services involved. Feedback and follow-up procedures would be beneficial (see the Community Resource Profile on page 29).

The school may need to access services such as counselling, parent education programs, mediation, leisure and recreation activities, before- and after-school care and legal aid. Services the school may wish to make part of their network include:

- Department of Health and Community Services
- local police (Police in Schools program)
- medical practitioner
- family support services
- pastoral care team from the Catholic Education Office
- guidance officers from the Directorate of Schools Education
- Safety House
- psychologists in private practice
- educational consultants in private practice
- appropriate resources and services for students and parents from different cultural and religious backgrounds.

CHECKLIST

Leadership and management practices (school structure)

Structure here implies the organisational and leadership practices that take place in classrooms, in the playground and school community, and among staff, students and parents. The checklist below has been devised to assist your school in creating structures that will help build a safe-school ethos.

Does the school provide:

- ❏ structures – such as the Student Representative Council, classroom meetings and Quality Circles – for students to voice their problems and concerns and to explore ways in which these can be resolved?

- ❏ structures that give students opportunity to develop leadership skills, such as in buddy programs, a Welcoming Committee, peer mediation?

- ❏ sufficient time, resources and acknowledgment for the student welfare team to work at the levels of both intervention and prevention?

- ❏ opportunities to build constructive partnerships – such as teacher–teacher, student–student, teacher–student – throughout the school community?

- ❏ avenues for building relationships with the parent community?

- ❏ professional development for all staff so they can effectively support and implement best practice for a safe environment throughout all areas of the school?

- ❏ a learning environment that is equitable and inclusive for all teachers and students?

- ❏ a network of outside professionals to whom teachers, students and parents can go for additional support and services?

- ❏ sufficient support and encouragement to teachers, which will allow them to take on positions of leadership in a dynamic fashion?

COMMUNITY RESOURCE PROFILE

NAME OF AGENCY: ....

CONTACT PERSON: ....

ADDRESS: ....

.... Postcode: ....

PHONE: .... FAX: ....

E-MAIL: ....

PROGRAMS OFFERED:

....

....

....

PROGRAMS SUITABLE FOR: (please circle)

Students   Teachers   Parents   Student welfare staff

DURATION OF PROGRAM(S):

....

....

....

REFERRAL PROCEDURE:

....

....

....

ADDITIONAL NOTES:

....

....

....

....

CHAPTER 4

Playground supervision

Playground supervision can be a time of distress for teachers. They often spend their time endeavouring to solve the problems and conflicts that are brought to them by students who feel hurt, angry and upset. Listening for their concerns on a noisy, busy playground is a challenge. Rogers (1994) suggests that 20 per cent of the student's day is spent in the playground. Fuller et al. indicate that the level of bullying peaks at lunchtime, is less frequent at morning recess and occurs least often in the classroom (Fuller, Graff & McGraw, cited in Fuller, 1998).

What can we, as teachers, do to make the school playground a safe and happy place for all students? Below are activities that your school may implement to engage and support your students at recess and lunchtime; this will help with the teachers' task of playground supervision.

Wet-day timetable

When students are kept inside due to inclement weather, problems with supervision are more likely to arise. Students need to let off steam, whether actively or passively. Practical and safe activities need to be made available to all students to avoid lunchtime chaos.

Some suggestions are given below.

- Invite students to bring in board and card games from home to leave at school during the wet months. Younger students could bring in activity books. All these materials could be used to create a games library in the classroom.
- Teach a variety of games that require little space and virtually no equipment. Some examples are noughts and crosses, SOS, charades, hangman, 20 questions.
- Provide drawing materials.
- Invite students to bring along magazines about sport, music and computers to share with the class.
- Allocate an area in the school where students can be active — a multi-purpose room or gym that is supervised.
- Have simple activities of art and craft in the art room, which need no or little instruction. This will require supervision.
- Have the library open at lunchtime. Many teachers express the view that the library is often a safe haven for students who are being bullied.
- Send older students to the junior rooms to read the students stories, teach them songs, dances and games.

Lunchtime interest groups

To encourage a lunchtime interest for those students who are isolated and friendless in the playground, a supervised area could be set aside so they could engage with other students through sharing a common activity. Playground survival can be particularly challenging for older boys in Years 4–6 who do not like playing team sports or who have difficulty in gross motor co-ordination. They can become an easy target for bullying. Some ideas students have come up with are:

- gardening club
- art/craft club
- chess club
- group interested in computers.

Students will have many more ideas. Such groups may meet weekly, fortnightly or monthly, depending on the time and resources available. The school may wish to enlist the help of parents.

> One parent had shared with us her Year 5 son's longing for a wet-day timetable. He enjoyed school better when it was a wet-day timetable because he could stay inside and draw. Drawing was his forte; he was affirmed and acknowledged for his drawing skill. Lunchtimes otherwise became a time when he was labelled, teased, excluded and victimised because the boys thought he was 'nerdy' at sport. The consequence of this was sitting with the girls at lunchtime, talking about shows on the television. This created other repercussions.

Perhaps if the school had set up a drawing club that met on a regular basis, the boy's self-esteem might not have suffered so greatly. This would have helped him find a niche in the school.

Layout of school grounds

The school playground should be a safe place and have a sense of 'green', providing as much diversity for play as possible. Passive and active areas need to be defined, so that students can enjoy playing alone or in groups. They need to feel safe and secure and know that they are being watched by the teacher on playground duty. Does your school provide:

- a sense of 'green' – shrubs, garden beds, trees and flowers?
- colourful wall murals?
- safe adventure playground equipment?
- seating in quiet areas?
- sports areas – for basketball, netball, handball, four square, football and so on – that are separate from other play areas?
- a shaded sand-play area?
- painted activities on the ground (hopscotch, four square)?

Staff

Teachers agree that the worst days for supervision are on hot days, windy days and wet days. Schools also report that Mondays are often difficult for those students who have spent the weekend with the non-custodial parent. Some schools may wish to put on an extra staff member on such days. It is extremely important that teachers be punctual for their supervision duty.

Availability of sports equipment

Keeping students actively engaged at lunchtime and recess reduces boredom and frustration. These emotions can trigger anti-social behaviour such as bullying. If possible, it's a good idea to teach games that are inclusive and develop a sense of co-operation between the students. It is also important to consider the type of sports equipment that would best serve your students.

Split lunchtime, shortened recess and lunchtime breaks

Some very large schools may consider having a split lunchtime with two separate times allocated for lunch to avoid crowding and boredom due to lack of availability of sports equipment. Some schools have also opted for shorter recess and lunchtime breaks and finishing school earlier.

Spot checks

Trouble spots need to be checked regularly, even the toilets. This can be effective, saving tedious investigation of an incident at a later date. Regular spot checks send a positive message to students that teachers are attentive to bullying.

Vulnerable students

Vulnerable students need to be reminded to play where they can be seen. Initially, a short-term measure may be walking or playing near the teacher on yard duty.

Staff briefing

Teachers may need to be briefed about students who are being victimised, for example: where the bullying is occurring, the type of bullying, the students involved and current strategies that are being employed. This shifts the sole responsibility away from the classroom teacher to one of shared responsibility, which is in keeping with a whole-school ethos.

Three-tier lunch break

The 'Sandwich Lunch' is a metaphor used to describe the three-tier lunch break, which has been devised by Marcella Reiter (Excellence in Learning, Living and Achieving) for students with social and emotional needs. This structure helps manage challenging playground behaviour. It is something like a sandwich consisting of two slices of bread and a filling of free choice in the middle:

First third The student engages in a set structured activity (always in view of the teacher doing playground supervision). This activity can be a game, sporting activity, peer or buddy project, school maintenance task, gardening and so on. The activities selected should be ones that make the student feel proud and enhance self-esteem.

Second third The student has free time and participates in an activity of his or her choice.

Final third Again, the student engages in a structured activity, either a continuation of the first third or something different.

As the student practises and develops the necessary social skills to interact appropriately, the 'bread' and 'filling' stages of the 'Sandwich Lunch' can be switched, that is first third – free play, second third – structured activity, final third – free play. This format remains in place until such time as the teacher feels confident that the student has sufficient skills to behave appropriately in the playground.

CHECKLIST

Considerations for playground supervision

It would be unrealistic to think that the teachers on playground supervision are fully responsible for the behaviour of students during this time. All students and all teachers are responsible in making recess and lunchtime a positive social experience for all.

A supervision checklist has been devised to assist schools in building a safe and supportive environment for all students.

As a staff do we:

- ❑ arrive for yard duty supervision at the correct and allocated time?

- ❑ supervise the toilets and recognised hot spots?

- ❑ take positive action to encourage isolated students to join a peer group?

- ❑ provide students with a repertoire of strategies to handle playground conflict for themselves?

- ❑ provide enough playground/sports equipment for positive play?

- ❑ teach non-competitive and inclusive games?

- ❑ provide targeted students with a variety of appropriate strategies other than just telling them to 'ignore them and walk away'?

- ❑ provide students with the skills to ask for help?

- ❑ follow through on a reported incident?

- ❑ provide individual playground plans for students who experience difficulty in the playground?

- ❑ get briefed regarding students who are being victimised in the playground?

Most importantly, does the school reflect an ethos that says we're committed to making playground play a positive and social experience for all students? When bullying reports are made, are they taken seriously and dealt with promptly?

CHAPTER 5

Dealing with a bullying incident

It is important for a school's stance on bullying to be transparent to all in the community, and to let it be known in particular instances that action is 'being taken' in a spirit of resolution and restitution. When a school is unclear about its course of action and underlying beliefs, the likelihood of incidents becoming prolonged, persistent and serious is increased. When this occurs parents unfortunately may seek legal action as their best possibility. Most Australian schools are sensitive to the issue and take the necessary steps so that such a course of action does not become a reality in their school community.

Studies have shown that a reduction in school violence occurs when a whole-school approach is adopted. A whole-school approach provides a solid, supportive foundation so that the challenges can more effectively be met. When prevention strategies are thus implemented, maintained and evaluated, the need for intervention is reduced.

Inevitably school bullying does and will exist, as part of our human nature is to experiment with and explore the use of power; for some this unfortunately becomes an abuse of power. Schools, however, can be pro-active and instrumental in reducing the frequency of this occurring. This is difficult to achieve if values and attitudes in the school community reflect the belief that bullying is a necessary part of growing up and a pre-requisite for character building and that students should sort out the bullying themselves. This is not only damaging for the target of bullying but the beliefs perpetuate a bullying ethos in the school.

Never should students be left to 'sort it out themselves' in an unsupported manner nor should teachers deal with the issue in an isolated context. When this is the prevailing ethos in the school, the so-called solutions are short-sighted and short-lived. It is crucial to make the shift away from focusing on the actions and consequences of individuals in isolated incidents and on to viewing the issue in a whole-school context.

Unfortunately there is no quick fix or simple solution. We need to consider first the school environment and how its implicit values, beliefs, attitudes and current practices have influence within and throughout the school community. Members of the school community can then explore collaboratively best practices and procedures to deal with a bullying incident. When an agreed set of procedures is in place, teachers feel supported to act confidently and consistently.

Diagram 6 illustrates the importance of creating a positive and effective learning and social environment for all students. By creating such a solid base, the need for intervention practices is reduced.

When working with students involved in long-term bullying (whether it be the target, a bystander or the bully), it is imperative that teachers and administrators first question:

- leadership practices
- management practices
- level of supervision in place
- prevention strategies

ALL students require a positive and supportive learning environment.
This occurs when the school provides:

- shared values, beliefs and attitudes in the school community

- an environment of mutual support and respect

- quality relationships fostered between teacher and teacher, student and teacher, student and student

- an established discipline policy that is well publicised and practised

- quality playground supervision

- avenues for students to voice concerns and formulate solutions

- shared classroom management strategies

- shared playground management strategies

- clearly delineated leadership structures for students and teachers

- an inclusive and equitable classroom.

PREVENTION

ALL students benefit when curriculum teaches life skills that
resolve and diffuse conflict:

- conflict resolution
- empathy training
- assertiveness training

- negotiation and mediation skills
- problem-solving.

PREVENTION

SOME students need a more specific vehicle for dealing with
conflict and other difficulties related to bullying. These include:

- No Blame Approach (pages 38–40) or Method of Shared Concern (pages 40–43)

- logical consequences (page 43)

- time-out (page 43)

- an individual student management plan (page 44).

INTERVENTION

A FEW students require:

- counselling   • suspension   • expulsion.

INTERVENTION

Diagram 6 Moving from prevention to intervention strategies.

CHECKLIST

Responding to a bullying incident

There is no simple or quick-fix solution when dealing with a bullying incident. If the school community has built a solid foundation of beneficial curriculum and effective leadership and management practices with the focus on prevention, intervention in many cases may not be necessary. Individual and isolated solutions are often short-term and short-lived.

The checklist below has been devised to assist schools in dealing with bullying incidents using a whole-school approach.

Prevention

❑ Does the school encourage and maintain a climate of respect?

❑ Does the school reflect leadership and management practices that contribute to building a safe and supportive learning environment for all students?

❑ Does the school curriculum develop life skills to nurture personal development in an inclusive and equitable manner?

❑ Does the school have a well-publicised student management policy or discipline policy that is practised by all?

❑ Has each class devised its own set of classroom rules?

❑ Does the school have playground rules that are understood and practised by all school members?

Intervention

❑ Are staff members committed to a common response to bullying when incidents occur?

❑ Does the school adopt a philosophy that moves away from punishment to resolution?

❑ Are there clear guidelines outlining the responsibilities of teachers when dealing with a bullying incident?

❑ Does the student management policy outline corrective procedures, for example, time-out, logical consequences (see page 43), denial of privileges, developing and implementing an individual student management plan, suspension and expulsion?

❑ Do teachers speak respectfully and directly with those concerned in the incident?

❑ Do teachers follow up and follow through on the incident?

❑ Do teachers provide students with opportunities to discuss and explore possible solutions that may resolve the issue?

❑ Are students and families resourced with appropriate services in the community as necessary?

- intervention strategies
- grievance procedures
- level of outside professional help accessed
- current anti-bullying policy.

Reviewing the above practices places the issue of intervention in a more realistic perspective. Without the necessary organisational structures, level of supervision, curriculum components and other preventative strategies in place, the issue of intervention becomes paramount. As teachers and educators, can we shift the focus away from intervention to one of prevention using a whole-school approach?

Moralistic, legalistic and humanistic approaches to a bullying incident

The following pages outline a variety of approaches to handling a bullying incident, ranging from non-punitive to punitive approaches. By collaboratively establishing an agreed set of procedures within the framework of the whole school, consistency and confidence is increased for all members of the school community.

Rigby (1996) has grouped these into three approaches, listing advantages and disadvantages. These are:
- the moralistic approach
- the legalistic approach
- the humanistic approach.

The moralistic approach

The moralistic approach is when students are expected to abide by the school's values (Rigby, 1996). Following is a possible scenario that illustrates this:

> The student who has been bullying is sent to a senior teacher who outlines the school's stand on bullying. The student is then asked to write an essay outlining the values that have been violated, which the principal may check. The bully may also be asked to write a letter of apology to the bullied student.

Advantages of this approach
- It promotes school values.
- It appeals to the student's sense of morality.

Disadvantages of this approach
- The bully's motives are ignored.
- The bully may seek reprisal in forms more difficult to diagnose.

The legalistic approach

With this approach the perpetrator of bullying is aware of a list of rules with a set of consequences or sanctions that range in severity.

Advantages of this approach

- It is a quick method.
- Students can recognise what is acceptable behaviour.
- Punishment can be administered according to the seriousness of the behaviour.

Disadvantages of this approach

- It is a short-term solution only; there is no reconciliation of the perpetrator with the bullied student.
- It may be time-consuming pinpointing the details of the behaviour so the correct sanction can be administered.
- It may have little impact on the persistent bullies.
- The bully seeks retribution for his or her punishment in covert and insidious ways.

The humanistic approach

The focus of this approach is to bring about a change in the thinking and behaviour of the student who is bullying. The teacher does not seek to lay blame or apply punishment but genuinely listens, steering the student towards appropriate behaviour and feasible solutions. It is important that the teacher creates a non-threatening style of communication with a sincere attempt to understand the bully at a more personal level (Rigby, 1996).

Advantages of this approach

- The bully makes a change in his or her behaviour and thinking rather than finding another student to target.
- Solutions can become long-term.
- It repairs the relationship between the bully and the target.

Disadvantages of this approach

- Some teachers may feel uncomfortable adopting this approach because it is focused on the solution rather than on punishment or blame.
- It is time-consuming.
- Parents may think that the school is not taking a 'hardline' in dealing with the issue.

To give a clearer understanding of the humanistic approach we here outline two procedures: the No Blame Approach, devised by Barbara Maines and George Robinson (video,1992) in England, and the Method of Shared Concern, the work of Anatol Pikas, Swedish psychologist. These methods have been used in Europe and in a growing number of schools in Australia.

The No Blame Approach

Bullying is here addressed by establishing a support group of bullies and/or bystanders involved in a particular incident. A problem-solving approach is used, which gives responsibility rather than blame to the group. The group reports back at regular meetings. The seven steps in the procedure are outlined below (Cowie, Sharp & Smith, ch. 5, in Sharp & Smith, 1994a).

Step 1 Interview the target of the bullying

The teacher interviews the bullied student to find out about his or her feelings. The teacher does not need to know all about the incident but does need to know who is involved. Permission must be gained from the bullied student to tell the bullies how he or she is feeling about the incident. The target is reassured that the bullies will not be in trouble so there is no concern for reprisal.

Step 2 Convene a meeting with the students involved

An informal but powerful peer situation is being established. The main bullies, bystanders and colluders are included. This may be a small group of six students who meet together with the teacher separately from the target. The support group often needs reassurance at the beginning of the meeting that they are not in trouble. The teacher explains that they have been chosen as they can all offer help in some way. This is what the group has in common.

An informal atmosphere is created by arranging seating in a circular fashion and, if possible, using a room that is neutral ground for those involved.

Step 3 Share with the group the target's feelings

The teacher shares indirectly how the bullied student is feeling, not apportioning blame with details of the actual incident. The teacher may have a poem, story, drawing or diary entry done by the target to illustrate how she or he feels. (Research indicates that effective education for bullies is empathy training.) The teacher's aim is to raise empathy within the group, asking questions such as: 'Has anyone ever been bullied at school?'.

The teacher listens to the students' responses, suggesting that the target must be feeling like that too. The teacher does not ask *why* questions. In the end it serves only to waste time and distracts students from offering solutions.

Step 4 Hand over responsibility to the group

The teacher emphasises in a non-judgmental way that everyone has the right to feel safe and happy at school. The teacher reassures the group that they can support the target, thus handing over the responsibility to them. The focus becomes the solution not the blame.

Step 5 Ask the group for their ideas and solutions

The teacher asks students to suggest ways that they could make the bullied student feel happier at school. The teacher then offers approving comments but does not extract a promise from the students regarding their solutions. Students' suggestions may include:
• I'll invite him to join in our game.
• I'll ask if she wants to join our group at lunchtime.

It is advised to ignore negative and resentful comments, and to focus on praising suggestions offered from the group. This often reassures the quieter students to make a contribution or to reinforce someone else.

Some teachers believe including a couple of responsible students (who may be in leadership roles) can help raise the social conscience of the group and the flow of the process.

Step 6 Let the students implement their plan

The teacher ends the meeting by giving the students the responsibility to solve the problem and together develop a plan. It is vital that the responsibility is passed on to the group, encouraging ownership in terms of implementing the plan. The teacher expresses confidence in the group and arranges a time and place to follow up and review the situation with each student individually.

Step 7 Follow-up interviews with each student

As arranged, the teacher meets with each of the students a week later to review solutions. It is best to check in with the target first. The teacher ascertains whether the bullying has stopped. If so, each student is complimented and thanked. Reviews can be continued for as long as required. Usually two reviews are adequate.

What students think of the No Blame Approach

When Maines and Robinson (video,1992) interviewed students who experienced this approach, comments went like this:

Good way to solve problems without getting hassled.
Surprised we weren't punished.
At first I didn't want to be involved but when I wasn't in trouble it was okay.
Teacher didn't have to take sides because they didn't ask what happened.

When the focus is not on blame or punishment students can relax, which puts them in a better frame of mind to identify how the target feels and offer possible solutions.

What educators think of the No Blame Approach

This approach needs thoughtful and careful direction to arouse empathy in students. Empathy brings about changes of heart and in behaviour. If this approach is not steered appropriately, students can become cynical and undermine the approach.

Method of Shared Concern

The Method of Shared Concern (Cowie, Sharp & Smith, ch. 5, in Sharp & Smith, 1994a) uses a non-confrontational counselling style, with the primary focus being to find a solution. The aim is to enable the target and the bully to function peacefully within the same school, not to develop a friendship.

The Method of Shared Concern comprises three stages:
1 individual interviews with the bullies followed by an interview with the target
2 follow-up discussions with each of the students to evaluate progress
3 group discussion with all students concerned.

The role of the teacher is to:

- find a quiet place away from the classroom so that the interview can be held in private
- listen to each student without judgment or blame
- refrain from 'trying to get to the bottom of it'
- remain empathic during the interview, allowing students enough time to say what they need to
- create a positive climate during the interview by arranging chairs in a non-confrontational manner
- steer students towards positive outcomes
- document the incident and solutions offered
- inform necessary parties, such as parents and other teachers
- follow up and follow through with the students concerned.

Stage 1 First meeting: interviews with the bullies

Each bully is interviewed separately. The teacher commences with the ringleader as he or she carries the most power and control within the group.

When the student is seated and looking at the teacher, the issue is raised of the target having difficulty being at school. The teacher might start with a statement such as, 'Susie is having a hard time at school lately' (indirect), said in an assertive tone, or 'I hear you've been nasty to Susie. Tell me about it' (direct). This is said assertively but in a non-judgmental manner.

No matter in which way the bully chooses to respond, the teacher does not engage in blame or interrogation, or waste time asking the student *why* questions as often students do not know why they have engaged in negative behaviours. It is the teacher's role at this point to voice concern about Susie. And it is at this point that there is usually an expression of concern and admission that he or she was involved in the situation.

Next the teacher asks the student, 'I was wondering what you could do to help Susie in this situation?'

It is important that the teacher waits for the student to come up with solutions, then gives encouragement and praise. The teacher comments by saying, 'Great, you try that out for the week and we'll check out what's been happening when I see you on … (date)'.

In some cases students are reluctant to offer solutions and suggestions. The teacher may need to make suggestions with which the student feels comfortable, for example: 'I've got an idea that may be useful, I'd like to tell you about it'.

Difficulties that may arise when interviewing the bully

According to Sharp and Smith (1994a), students may:

- be unable to offer solutions. The teacher then offers solutions in a supportive manner
- not want to take responsibility for the problem. The teacher continues to work on raising empathy without bringing blame to the situation
- be unco-operative and silent. The teacher waits silently for the students to speak
- offer solutions that are ineffective. The teacher leads the students to see if the solutions offered would stop the bullying.

Interview with the target (Stage 1 continued)

After speaking with the bullies, the target is interviewed.

When the target feels comfortable, the teacher begins the interview with,

'How have things been going? I hear some unpleasant things have been happening to you'.

The target will generally discuss how he or she has been feeling and what has been taking place. This allows the teacher to ascertain the type of victim behaviour the target has been experiencing: the classic, provocative, passive or colluding (see Lesson 1, page 70). Together the target and teacher can explore solutions and strategies and establish what action will be taken.

Remember:

At this stage it is important to remain patient and supportive. For many students who have been targeted, it has taken considerable courage to finally tell. Their need to be heard and reassured that resolution will take place is crucial.

Stage 2 Follow-up meeting

At this stage the teacher meets with each student separately to find out how she or he has been going with their proposed course of action. If the bullying persists, the teacher continues to work with the students individually to further foster an understanding of the target's position and his or her feelings as well so that a suitable solution can be formulated. If it has stopped, the teacher reminds the students to continue in this manner and informs them individually that a group meeting will be held at a designated date.

Remember:

Congratulate students when they have followed through on their strategies and solutions.

Stage 3 Final meeting

This final meeting is important. The key purpose is to maintain the changes in behaviour that have occurred and allow students to behave congenially towards the target.

Preparation allows for better results, thus it is best to meet with the bullying students first, allowing them to prepare what positive comments they can say to the target. The teacher then invites the target, supporting him or her as they all sit comfortably together.

The teacher briefly discusses how well the situation has improved and asks the students how they can maintain this situation, steering towards a positive agreement between both parties of how they can behave in the future.

Remember:

The target can sit next to the teacher for moral support.

Another meeting is then arranged in six weeks for reviewing the situation.

What teachers think of the Method of Shared Concern

- The students involved are more relaxed because of the consultative nature of the interview.

- With the focus on solutions rather than blame, the bullies involved often express relief because *they are not in trouble!*
- Teachers prevent secondary victimisation from occurring by indirectly giving the message that the target did not tell. The method always commences with the bullies being interviewed first. This prevents anger and reprisal being directed to the target.
- Teachers interviewing the bullies individually experience better quality communication: the students can speak more freely and honestly.
- Teachers become more tuned in to the types of victim behaviour the target is displaying and can better determine whether he or she has contributed to the situation.
- Teachers feel relieved that they need not get bogged down in asking the students *why* questions because this can become a bottomless pit.

Using other approaches

The teacher may have used the humanistic approach (No Blame Approach or the Method of Shared Concern as outlined on pages 38–43) and found that this was not effective for resolving that particular incident. It may have served as a good starting point, but other strategies need to be employed if the bullying is serious and persistent.

Rigby (1996) bases his definition of seriousness on five key points:
- How distressed is the victim?
- To what extent are the parents concerned? (This is usually an indicator of the child's distress.)
- How long has the bullying been going on?
- How willing is the perpetrator to acknowledge the hurt that has been caused?
- To what degree is the perpetrator ready to work towards resolution?

Keeping the above points in mind, and if serious enough, it may be necessary in some situations to move from a non-punitive to a punitive approach that increases in severity accordingly.

Other intervention strategies may include:
- logical consequences. Students need to be made aware that their behaviour is related to an outcome (Rogers, 1998). It has consequences which will affect themselves and others
- time-out. Removing the student out of the group (Glasser, 1969). It is not seen as a punishment but as a time when he or she can think about their behaviour and offer a solution
- denial of privileges, with the opportunity to redeem one's self
- individual student management plan (see page 44)
- parental involvement (see pages 58–65)
- counselling
- removal of the bully away from the target into another class
- suspension
- expulsion.

School-based counselling

Schools have a wide variety of talents among staff members. Teachers who are interested in student welfare often volunteer their time in a school-based counselling role.

Some schools have steered away from using the word 'counsellor' and have preferred to adopt titles such as Care Co-ordinator, Welfare Co-ordinator and Pastoral Care Adviser.

Teachers in this role appreciate that every student in the school deserves to have at least one person on staff with whom they feel safe and comfortable when discussing their personal problems. If students see that a set structure exists and is user-friendly, their needs can be met more effectively.

Many teachers in this role may not have formal qualifications in counselling but draw on their years of experience and empathic communication style. Kids Help Line (1996) states that it is vital that the teacher or counsellor explain how he or she works and reassure the student that confidentiality will be maintained. The skills required in this role are having the empathy to find out how the student is feeling and thinking, showing respect and giving appropriate and relevant information. Students may wish to approach the school counsellor voluntarily or may be recommended by their class teacher 'to chat' with the counsellor.

If the students' needs go beyond the skill of the school-based counsellor, it is then important to use the correct protocol and procedures for referring these students and their families to the appropriate outside agencies (see 'Building a network', pages 27–8).

Individual student management plan

An individual student management plan (see pages 146–8):
- is an adjunct to a well-developed student management policy
- is the result of negotiation between teacher(s) and student (Rogers, 1998)
- needs to be simple, measurable, reliable and set within a time frame.

An individual student management plan must state:
- *what* is the behaviour goal for that student
- *where* the behaviours have occurred and are occurring
- *how* to achieve this plan
- *when* to start the plan.

Before implementing a plan it is advised that the teacher monitors the negative behaviour and discusses this behaviour with the student in a non-judgmental manner, also that the teacher meets with the parents for discussion. The rationale behind an individual student management plan is that the student can grow in self-reliance and self-discipline through a process that:
- is oriented to problem-solving
- explores alternatives
- gives choice, developing the skills of decision-making
- requires commitment from the student and the teacher (Rogers, 1998).

The benefits of an individual student management plan are that it:
- fosters creative thinking and problem-solving
- gives the student the opportunity to make a commitment
- empowers the student to become responsible for his or her actions
- gives the student the experience of making a choice, hence developing the process of deliberation, decision-making and planning.

Suspension

Suspension may give the school community the message that the issue of bullying is taken seriously. Teachers and principals, however, need to consider not only their legal and pastoral responsibilities but also those of the parents. During this period the student requires a suitable learning program. The student welfare team will need to develop a plan to monitor, evaluate and support the student when returning to the classroom. Ongoing support and monitoring are essential.

Expulsion (negotiated transfer)

Expulsion is a severe disciplinary measure that is reserved for serious circumstances. Many issues need to be considered when such steps are taken. It is important that schools work through appropriate processes prior to taking such a measure.

In summary

When schools are required to intervene, clear guidelines on agreed intervention practices are necessary. Regardless of the school's agreed practice, it is important that all teachers understand that their role influences the outcome of the incident.

Teachers can de-escalate the incident, bringing about resolution and restitution, or escalate the situation creating secondary victimisation for the target when handled incorrectly. Rigby (1996) and Slee found that in the cases reported 50 per cent made no improvement and 7 per cent became worse. These alarming statistics stress the importance of teachers needing to know how to handle bullying incidents (the agreed practice) and why this procedure is adopted (the understanding based on shared values and beliefs).

The school must keep in mind that whatever the procedure adopted it must:
- protect the bullied student
- deter others engaging in bullying behaviour
- allow the bully to change his or her behaviour in a positive way.

Based on these three requirements the staff, through a collaborative process, may choose to mix the methods to come to a procedure that is effective for the school.

Monitoring incidents of bullying

The entire staff may wish to establish a formal monitoring system so that incidents of bullying can be logged. Below are some issues to consider.
- Designing a pro-forma report form that is acceptable to all staff members.
- Does the format include report forms each for the teacher and the student?
- Where will this report live? in the student's file? in a separate file?
- How will information on the report form be communicated back to the teachers who need to be involved?

On pages 46–7 are two sample report forms you may wish to use for your school (one each for teachers and for students).

BULLYING INCIDENT REPORT

(for completion by teacher)

Date of report: ....   Teacher completing report: ....   Signature: ....

DETAILS OF REPORT	SOLUTIONS OFFERED BY STUDENTS	TEACHER FOLLOW-UP
Where incident occurs?		Teacher to follow up: .... Review date: .... People who need to be informed:
Who is involved?		
How long has the bullying been occurring?		
What happened?		Comments:

Bullying: A Whole-school Approach, ACER Press, © Copyright 2001 Amelia Suckling and Carla Temple

BULLYING: STUDENT REPORT FORM

STUDENT'S NAME: ....

DATE: ....

TEACHER HANDLING REPORT: ....

The teachers at our school will do their best to help you deal with bullying problems. Sharing your thoughts and feelings about the problem will help us find the best way to deal with it.

Who is involved?

....
....
....
....

Where does it happen?

....
....
....
....

What happened?

....
....
....
....

How can we solve the problem?

....
....
....
....

Bullying: A Whole-school Approach, ACER Press, © Copyright 2001 Amelia Suckling and Carla Temple

CHAPTER 6

Developing an anti-bullying policy

What is an anti-bullying policy?

An anti-bullying policy becomes part of and relevant to the school's existing discipline policy, student welfare policy, pastoral care policy, student management policy or code of conduct (some of the many names used in schools). It provides a framework for how to tackle bullying.

Importance of an anti-bullying policy

An anti-bullying policy gives the school community clear expectations, direction, commitment and consistency in tackling bullying behaviour. Such a document gives the school the opportunity to state clearly that bullying in any form will not be tolerated and will be dealt with seriously rather than viewing it as an inevitable part of school life.

The policy assists schools to move beyond a crisis management approach to adopting strategies of prevention and intervention.

Characteristics of an anti-bullying policy

Sharp and Thompson advise that the features below be considered when formulating policy (ch. 3 in Sharp & Smith, 1994a).

A clear, firm statement regarding the school's stand on anti-bullying

This illustrates the school's commitment to anti-bullying strategies and procedures.

A definition of bullying in its many forms

It is important that bullying behaviour can be identified by students, teachers and parents and that the school community share this understanding (see pages 69–70).

Prevention strategies to be adopted by the school

Implementing prevention strategies throughout the school is essential if the need for intervention is to be reduced. Consider how effective playground supervision (pages 30–33), wise use of curriculum (pages 12–19) and school management and leadership practices (pages 20–28) can be used to build a school ethos that reflects an anti-bullying stand.

ity (parents, teachers and students) go

s bullying cannot be reduced without reporting of
dents by making it school knowledge on how to
rt. Parents also need to know the protocol involved
eir child. Some schools design report forms to assist
eport forms). Then teachers will need to decide who
through on the report (see page 46).

t

hool community know how to deal with bullying. Do
use when confronted with bullying? (These are given
to support and help their child to handle bullying (see
eans and/or support them if they are the bully?
adopting a shared best practice? (See Chapter 5, pages

teachers, parents and students to uphold the

e in our school community, what is each member's
any schools are including a statement outlining the
g something to the effect that it is the responsibility of
orm) to make a report.

olicy

heir policy to assess its effectiveness within the school
pproximately every 18 months–2 years) the same ques-
so on they have done previously, noting the changes in
the data. It is also important to consider what indicators to look for that reflect a shift in the
school's values and practices as a result of the policy.

It is important to keep the language in the document clear and easily understood, remembering that it will be read by students, teachers and parents.

It is not necessary to detail everything in this document; flexibility is important. Rigby (1996, p. 140) believes that 'it may indeed be sensible sometimes for a school not to "show its hand" entirely in policy statement'.

Exploring a consultative approach for policy development

There are many important issues the school must address prior to developing a whole-school policy on anti-bullying. The process for developing the policy is crucial and is just as important as the document itself. It can be slow and lengthy, requiring the nominated working team to be sensitive to the views of others and to investigate other policies and documents in the school that will have bearing on the anti-bullying policy, thus making sure all policies are aligned.

To reflect the values and ethos of the school community, teachers, non-teaching staff, students and parents all need to work through a consultative process to formulate a *living document* that expresses the school community's stand on bullying. Without involvement from the school community the final product may be merely window dressing.

The best place from which schools can start is to establish that bullying is totally unacceptable and will be dealt with seriously.

One school has built a reputation as the 'Telling School', as the principal impresses upon all new students that they have the right to attend school without fear of being bullied (St John Brooks, 1985, cited in Besag, 1989, p. 105).

To build a reputation as a 'telling school' requires that the school community shares a consciousness on what bullying is, the stand the school will take and acknowledges the measures adopted (prevention and intervention) to deal with the issue. This may require a shift in values and attitudes by members of the school community.

Steps in the consultative process

1 Acknowledgment

There needs to be acknowledgment that bullying exists in every school regardless of its location, religion, philosophy or its genuine concern of those within the school.

2 Raising awareness

The school community needs to keep abreast with up-to-date research and be given the opportunity to discuss key issues such as:

- what is bullying?
- what are the characteristics of a target? a perpetrator?
- how often do bullying incidents occur in the school?
- how does gender affect the incidence of bullying?
- what best practices are currently adopted worldwide?

Without raising awareness within the school, it is difficult for the school community to reach a shared vision.

3 Investigation

Teachers can administer surveys and questionnaires to determine the location, frequency and type of bullying experienced by students; also to determine to whom the students are reporting and how they are going about it.

Parents can be kept informed of survey results via newsletter updates. When appropriate, teachers can seek feedback from parents via the school newsletter and/or questionnaires.

Students Teachers can use a variety of avenues to receive feedback from their students.

4 Interpreting data

A working team needs to be established to comb through the results of the surveys and questionnaires. This should involve teachers, non-teaching staff, students and parents. Teachers may wish to invite parents personally or through requests for support as advertised in the school newsletter. The team should then set to answer if the data indicate:

- where the bullying takes place
- how frequently it occurs
- if students are reporting bullying
- what types of bullying occur most frequently.

5 Seeking solutions through strategies

When a school seeks the best solutions for addressing the issue of bullying, many aspects of the entire school community must be taken into account, and diverse avenues of resolution need to be explored.

Teachers

When defining strategies for their school culture, teachers must consider:

- management and organisational structures within the school community (teachers, non-teaching staff, students and parents), see Chapter 3, pages 20–29
- supervision (playground, corridor, classroom), see Chapter 4, pages 30-33
- curriculum, see Chapter 2, pages 12-19.

In terms of intervention practices, it is important that teachers agree on and are comfortable with using a set grievance procedure to deal with a bullying incident.

Parents

- Teachers send a questionnaire home to parents.
- Teachers conduct a carefully steered parent forum.

Students

Are students provided with an avenue to voice possible strategies and solutions via:

- Student Representative Council (page 25)?
- Quality Circles (pages 21–3)?
- classroom meetings (pages 20–21)?
- peer mediation (pages 24–5)?

6 Formulating a draft

The working team needs to formulate a draft policy (see pages 54–7 for guidelines for policy content) based on collated data and possible solutions and strategies as culled from the school community.

7 Reviewing the draft

The final policy may need to be drafted many times before it becomes the living document that reflects the values and ethos of the school community. The working team will be required to update staff frequently and staff will need to give feedback, and collaborate on key issues such as:

- the best possible procedure(s) for dealing with a bullying incident when it arises and how to report and record this
- the best possible strategies for building a preventative practice through consideration of playground management, curriculum and management and leadership within the school.

8 Implementing policy

The working team will need to plan with thought and care how and when the policy is to be implemented. Its success may depend on major changes such as the changing of the internal structure and management of the school. It may also depend on upgrading training of the staff in areas such as assertiveness, conflict resolution, peer mediation and counselling skills.

9 Celebration

Once the *when* and *how* of implementing the policy have been established, the school may wish to celebrate in a variety of ways:

- a launch night that involves the whole school community. The school may wish to invite the local press and media to inform the wider community of the school's stand on bullying
- publishing the policy in students' diaries
- giving a copy of the policy to every parent
- referring to the policy in the school's prospectus
- revisiting the policy at intervals via the school newsletter and inviting family discussion on various aspects, for example the ramifications of the bystander's behaviour.

Maintaining the policy

Reviewing and evaluating the policy are important steps in maintaining it as a living document. It is imperative that the policy be given a high profile so that it does not become a paper tiger. Keep the policy alive by regularly referring to it through:

- school assemblies
- newsletter updates
- slogans located in appropriate and significant places around the school
- keeping staff updated with current trends and practices
- ensuring all staff are responsible for upholding the policy
- students writing an anti-bullying code for display in their classroom and around the school (pages 92–4)
- students writing a bystanders' code for display in their classroom and around the school (pages 101–3)
- the Student Representative Council via role-plays, debates, artwork and so on at school assemblies and/or classroom visits
- informing new students, parents of new students and new staff of current policy.

Reviewing and evaluating policy

As we have seen, regular review is vital for keeping the policy relevant and effective for the school. Feedback may come from staff, students and parents. After a two-year period the surveys and questionnaires previously used to determine a reduction in the level of bullying can be re-administered. Other indicators of change to look for include:

- a decrease in the level of reported bullying
- increased enrolments
- a willingness from bystanders and parents to report bullying
- an earlier detection of bullying
- increased morale among students, teachers and parents
- less sick days taken by teaching and non-teaching staff
- less staff turnover
- less absenteeism among students
- a decrease in the duration of bullying.

Benefits of an anti-bullying policy

1 It provides parents with clear expectations on the school's approach to handling bullying.
2 It helps give the school a reputation for being pro-active in reducing bullying and taking the issue seriously.
3 It formalises the school's practices and procedures for the prevention and intervention of bullying, hence sharing one vision and approach.
4 It breaks down the secrecy code, which deters bullying behaviour from flourishing.
5 It raises community awareness by involving parents in formulating the policy.

It would be naive to believe that once the policy has been implemented immediate changes will occur. The effects of policy are seen in the long-term because the process is one of changing attitudes, values and relationships within the school community. The policy (through the process of consultation and documentation) becomes the *tool* for fostering change.

We have included an anti-bullying action plan (pages 54–7) to support your staff in formulating procedures and practices, from raising awareness through to implementing policy.

ANTI-BULLYING ACTION PLAN (1)

Finding Out About Bullying

AREAS FOR COLLABORATION	SHORT-TERM STRATEGIES	LONG-TERM STRATEGIES	COMMENTS
Raising staff awareness			
Surveying bullying in our school			
Raising student awareness of bullying			

ANTI-BULLYING ACTION PLAN (2)

Structure, Curriculum and Supervision

AREAS FOR COLLABORATION	SHORT-TERM STRATEGIES	LONG-TERM STRATEGIES	COMMENTS
Structure (management and leadership practices)			
Curriculum			
Supervision			

Bullying: A Whole-school Approach, ACER Press, © Copyright 2001 Amelia Suckling and Carla Temple

ANTI-BULLYING ACTION PLAN (3)

Dealing With a Bullying Incident

AREAS FOR COLLABORATION	SHORT-TERM STRATEGIES	LONG-TERM STRATEGIES	COMMENTS
Developing a reporting procedure			
Procedure for dealing with the incident			
Procedure for following up on the incident			

Bullying: A Whole-school Approach, ACER Press, © Copyright 2001 Amelia Suckling and Carla Temple

ANTI-BULLYING ACTION PLAN (4)

Policy Development

AREAS FOR COLLABORATION	SHORT-TERM STRATEGIES	LONG-TERM STRATEGIES	COMMENTS
Developing an anti-bullying policy (the content)			
Launching, implementing and maintaining the policy			
Evaluating the policy			

Bullying: A Whole-school Approach, ACER Press. © Copyright 2001 Amelia Suckling and Carla Temple

CHAPTER 7

The parents

When speaking with parents after conducting a parent information session, many have shared with us their responses to their child's being bullied and how they attempted to support their child in handling the behaviour. A selection of responses is listed below:

- *Just ignore them!*
- *Hit them back harder!*
- *Scream really loud when they come near you!*
- *Give them back the same medicine!*
- *Stick up for yourself!* (Often children do not know how they should do this.)
- Mum says, *Have the day off tomorrow!*
- Dad says, *Right, in the garage, I'll teach you to defend yourself!*
- *It's the school's fault. They never do anything about it. They're not tough enough on them!*
- *My kid is a bit like me. I was bullied at school too, and now it's happening to my child!*

In this chapter we aim to:

- consider the importance of building an ethos in the school that welcomes and works in partnership with parents.
- provide guidelines for conducting meetings with the parents of the bully and of the target.
- illustrate the importance of educating parents so that they can effectively support their children to handle peer conflict.

Working in partnership with parents

The key to tackling school bullying is creating a partnership between teachers, administrators, parents, students and the broader community. Due to the deceitful and complex nature of bullying, a multidimensional approach is crucial. Bullying cannot be stopped by teacher, student or parent working in isolation.

Building a partnership takes time, energy and integrity. Parents need to feel comfortable about working in partnership with the school in a variety of ways.

It is the school's role to invite and involve parents on both a formal and informal basis. Areas for parental involvement include:

- assisting in the classroom
- attending social functions
- open days
- drop-in centre within the school for parents to meet with other parents
- attending excursions with students
- parent committees

- family evenings
- newsletters
- parent education programs.

Parents are eager to add value to their children's lives and often seek avenues by which to do this. By offering a variety of parent education programs, schools can provide parents with the skills and knowledge to assist them in positively influencing their children. Such opportunities for parental involvement also help parents feel valued as members of the school community; they feel heard and acknowledged, whether it be to positively affirm, constructively criticise or share their concerns and fears relating to their child.

> 'Most families believe caring for their children and adolescents is the central objective of their lives. Most young people want to maintain a strong relationship with their parents , no matter how difficult that is. Many parents seek knowledge about how to parent more effectively and improve their relationship with their children.' (Suicide Prevention Victorian Task Force, July 1997, cited in Department of Education, Victoria, 1999)

What to expect when conducting a meeting with parents

Informing parents of bullying incidents or following through on a parent's request to deal with the bullying can be a daunting experience if one is unprepared and unsupported.

Bullying damages not only the targeted child but also his or her family. Teachers need to be aware and sensitive to the fact that the parents involved may have a different perception and understanding of the problem.

Parents of the targeted child may feel threatened and uncomfortable dealing with the issue for many reasons.

- They may have experienced the pain and discomfort of school bullying when they were children.
- They may believe the school has not dealt with the issue to their satisfaction and as a result are seeking legal advice.
- They may feel guilty and inadequate for not being able to give their child the skills to handle peer conflict.
- They may feel the school is responsible and wish to lay blame on specific teachers or administrators.

The parents of the bully may also feel threatened and uncomfortable.

- They may feel judged as having poor parenting skills and being inadequate role models for their child.
- They may feel angry for their child being *blamed*.
- They may believe it is a school issue that should not involve them as parents.
- They may value how their child has chosen to behave.

For any parent dealing with their child's bullying, it is an emotional and delicate issue. Parents will not feel clear and objective.

Teachers need to be prepared for all sorts of responses from the parents, which range widely. Below we list some, together with the effects such responses may have on their child.

- Ring up the parents of the children whom they believe are bullying their child, ready to lay blame and verbally abuse them, perhaps without knowing all the details of the incident. This may aggravate the problem and make it harder for their child.

- Tell their child to fight because that's how you stick up for yourself *but* the bully may be bigger, older, punch harder and have the support of a peer group.
- Tell their child to stay close to their friends *but* the child may not belong to a peer group and this reinforces his or her feelings of loneliness and isolation.
- Tell their child to run *but* the bully may run faster.
- Undermine their child's feelings about the incident by telling him or her it's a normal part of growing up and that 'it will toughen you up' *but* this compounds the child's feelings of helplessness and vulnerability.
- Tell their child to ignore it or avoid the bullies *but* the bullies are in the child's class and continually follow him or her around the playground, ready to tease and taunt.

The ideal is for the parent to approach the school so that together the parent and the child's teacher can work in partnership to bring about solutions.

The notes for parents on pages 63–5 may be photocopied for teachers to give to parents. These notes give parents some tips to share with their children. Teachers may wish to distribute these parent notes at their discretion, when a situation arises or they may be distributed at the commencement of the school year.

A teacher's role is crucial in determining the tone and outcome of the meeting. It is imperative that the problem does not become inflamed or escalate, creating secondary problems. Thus no teacher should be left to deal with the situation in isolation. A colleague should be present at these meetings: the principal, assistant principal, member from the student welfare team or another member of staff and, if necessary, outside professionals.

What to do when you *know* of the bullying incident

Be prepared

Prior to meeting with the parents, determine where the meeting will be conducted. A classroom is not always the best place to ensure privacy.

Also, collect as much information as possible. Do this discreetly without creating alarm or concern for those involved in the incident. (You may have information recorded on a report sheet.) For example:
- *where* the incident(s) took place
- *when* the incidents are occurring and how frequently
- *who* is involved (bully, target, bystanders)
- *what* the behaviours are
- *why* the bullying is occurring (it is important not to waste too much time on this question).

Speak to each set of parents separately. Prior to the parent meeting, organise with a colleague to sit in with you and record the minutes. This provides moral support and allows you to remain fully focused on the parents' concerns.

Guidelines

The purpose of this meeting is to seek solutions for restitution rather than blame, punishment and judgment.

1 Welcome the parents (or parent), they will feel nervous and uncomfortable, and allow time to put them at ease.

2 Thank the parents for coming. Many parents may have rearranged their work schedule to attend.

3 Establish with the parents that the purpose of the meeting is to offer support and develop a team approach for the betterment of their child (not to blame or criticise).

4 Express empathy for the parents (regardless of whether the child is the bully or the target).

5 Inform parents of the school's expectations of student behaviour and stand on bullying via the code of conduct and the anti-bullying policy.

6 Be sensitive to the parents' feelings when discussing the incident (no judgment or blame).

7 Listen to what the parents share about their child and the child's perception of the incident.

8 Discuss (sharing not telling) strategies that the school has implemented and/or is in the process of implementing.

9 Provide information about other agencies that offer professional support if required.

10 Record minutes of the meeting and read these back to the parents at the completion of the meeting so there are no misunderstandings.

11 Set a date for a follow-up meeting to review the situation.

Your school may wish to design a suitable pro-forma that will streamline the documentation of minutes and follow-up procedures. Ensure that the documentation is private and that the teachers concerned know where this is filed.

What to do when you *do not know* of the bullying incidents

Often parents approach the teacher with a bullying issue without the teacher being aware that this has been going on among his or her students. As mentioned previously (page 23), research indicates that if a child is to tell at all, the person they are least likely to inform is their teacher.

Being unaware of the problem can place teachers in a precarious position. The guidelines below will assist in steering the meeting towards a positive outcome.

1 Silently acknowledge the emotional climate of the meeting.

2 Being unaware of the situation, it is best to listen and be empathic.

3 Assure parents that you will investigate promptly and arrange a follow-up meeting.

4 Advise parents that time is required to follow up carefully and sensitively on the issue.

5 Respect the parents' version of their child's perception of the problem. You cannot make accurate comment or offer constructive solutions without knowing the details.

6 Assure parents that *together* you will work towards solutions and strategies to make school a safe and happy place for their child.

7 You may wish to share the school's stand on bullying and its current practices, procedures and strategies as documented in the school's anti-bullying policy.

8 Take minutes of the meeting.

9 Read the minutes back to the parents to ensure that there have been no misunderstandings.

10 Arrange for a follow-up meeting.

11 Inform the principal/student welfare team of the meeting and its outcome.

Preparing for a parent information session

Parents are keen to play an active role in educating their children in life skills. They want to be informed of the current trends in anti-bullying, have the opportunity to think about bullying in other ways and, most importantly, go away with a repertoire of strategies that they can use to help coach their children.

Devising a teacher's checklist will help in preparing for a parent information session. The questions to ask are:

What's to be done?   Who will do it?   When?

Here is a sample list of the tasks that may be entailed:
- staff meeting to decide who will oversee the session
- selecting date and time of session
- selecting a room/venue
- promoting the session
- sending a flyer to parents
- refreshments (yes/no)
- child minding (yes/no)
- signage
- meeting and greeting the parents before the session begins
- name tags
- photocopying parent information notes
- distributing parent information notes at the session
- cleaning up afterwards
- locking up.

Have fun, good luck!

FOR PARENTS:

Helping your child if he or she is bullying

Finding out your child is bullying at school can be alarming and unsettling for you as a parent; many emotions may surface. Find a time to talk quietly and calmly with your child. Here are some tips that may help you.

1 Listen carefully to your child, giving the message that you want to support him or her but that nobody deserves to be bullied.

2 If your child is bullying because of feeling angry, give support by encouraging him or her to channel the anger through: counting to ten, taking time out, bouncing a ball against a wall, listening to music or going for a run.

3 Help your child to understand that it's not always possible to have what one wants, and that he or she must be able to accept 'no' sometimes. Also encourage him or her to make distinctions between behaviours that are aggressive and those that are assertive, and to become clearer about the differences between coercion and negotiation, and co-operation and manipulation. You and your child's teacher can work on and clarify this together.

4 Help your child to understand that his or her behaviour has consequences for both himself/herself as well as others and that these may be hurtful to some.

5 Work in partnership with the school to support your child.

6 Here are some questions that may help the discussion with your child:
   • How are your friends going at school?
   • Who have you been playing with lately? What games do you and your friends like to play?
   • Are there any friends you don't feel good about? Is there anything you could do to change that?
   • Do you sometimes feel angry/sad/jealous/afraid and want to take your feelings out on others?
   • Is someone bullying you and making you feel upset and angry?
   • Are you being bossed around to bully other kids so you get to stay in their group?

7 While letting your child know you feel disappointed and that you strongly disapprove of bullying, remember that children learn best when praised for their efforts to make positive changes and when shown by adults better ways to behave. Therefore avoid punishing, blaming and shaming to bring about change in behaviour.

Bullying: A Whole-school Approach, ACER Press, © Copyright 2001 Amelia Suckling and Carla Temple

FOR PARENTS:

Helping your child to handle bullying

1 Listen carefully to your child. You may need to read between the lines to establish a clearer understanding of the bullying incident and your child's role in this.

2 Calmly ask your child how he or she has been handling the problem and together explore other possibilities.

3 Share with your child the message that nobody deserves to be bullied. Some children come to believe that they deserve the bullying because there is something wrong with them.

4 Offer to speak to your child's teacher in privacy without any fuss, even when your child retaliates and does not want you to intervene for fear of being labelled a dobber.

5 Meet your child at the classroom door at the end of a school day as this may offer support and protection. Before offering to do this, ask your child first. Some children may find this embarrassing or feel that it will escalate the problem. Many may find it helpful.

6 Discreetly be a social engineer on behalf of your child by encouraging new friendships at school and outside of school.

7 Advise your child to leave expensive items at home because this puts your child in a vulnerable position by having something that someone else does not have.

8 If your child does not belong to a peer group and is playing alone in the playground, tell him or her to play near the teacher on playground duty (a short-term solution).

9 Role-model and coach your child in developing confident body language. Body awareness is important and showing confident body language can act as a deterrent to becoming a target. Remind your child to stand tall, shoulders straight, make eye contact, arms by the sides and feet a little bit apart. A mirror is a great tool for practising a positive stance.

10 Rehearse one-liners with your child to help him or her cope with teasing. Here are some examples:

Yuck, you've got red hair.
That makes me easy to find in a crowd.

You look dumb, four-eyes.
Yeh, I've got an extra pair of eyes to check out everything that's going on.

Freak, big ears.
I can hear twice as good as you.

Have fun coming up with one-liners relevant to your child's circumstances. Endeavour to make them funny, surprising and brief and at all costs avoid remarks that will cause provocation and hostility. Rehearse these with your child, with attention given to body language and tone of voice.

11 Encourage your child to visualise a safety shield around him or herself. The shield looks like a clear plastic dome that goes all the way around and over the body, offering protection so that teasing and put-downs bounce back off.

12 Encourage your child to use positive self-talk and creative visualisation (that is, making pictures in the mind that are supportive) and to listen to positive self-talk statements that are affirming. Help your child to make friends with his or her thoughts. Examples of self-talk statements your child may use are:

'I can handle myself.'   'I'll give it a go.'   'It's okay to be different.'

Match this with positive pictures of him or herself to build inner strength. The mind is a dynamic tool for inner rehearsal that can support your child with his or her outer expression.

13 Encourage your child to use 'I' messages to support him or her in being assertive. Notice the difference when the response uses 'I' and when 'you' is used:
I don't like it when you talk to me that way. Stop it. (assertive)
Shut your mouth or I'll hit you. (aggressive)
You always say mean things to me, it's not fair. (passive)

14 Provide your child with picture story books for younger children and short chapter books for older children that address the issue of bullying through a variety of characters and story-lines. This helps your child to understand that bullying happens to many people, not to him or her alone. (Your local library or child's teacher will have a reading list.)

15 Believe your child when sharing with you that he or she is being bullied. Many children are reluctant to share this for fear of being blamed, misunderstood and labelled as a dobber or as having something wrong with them. Continue to share conversations and coach your child to come up with suitable alternatives.

PART TWO

PUTTING IT INTO PRACTICE

What is bullying?

Fact file

'Bullying is a form of aggressive behaviour which is usually hurtful and deliberate: it is often persistent, sometimes continuing for weeks, months or even years and it is difficult for those being bullied to defend themselves. Underlying most bullying behaviour is an abuse of power and a desire to intimidate and dominate.' (Sharp & Smith, 1994a, p. 1)

Rigby (1996) states that bullying contains seven key features. These are:

1 an intention to be hurtful
2 this intention is carried out
3 the behaviour harms the target
4 the bully overwhelms the target with his or her power
5 there is often no justification for the action
6 the behaviour repeats itself again and again
7 the bully derives a sense of satisfaction from hurting the target.

It is important that students understand that bullying comes in many forms. If they can identify the bullying behaviours, students can report more accurately what is happening and how they are affected.

Physical bullying

Physical bullying is fighting, kicking, punching, hitting, shoving, pinching, abusive gestures and moving in close on the target's personal space.

Verbal bullying

This is when the bully uses words in a malicious way to cause distress to another and thus feels powerful. Such forms of verbal bullying are teasing, swearing, using put-downs, spreading nasty rumours, and using stand-over tactics. Another form of verbal bullying is making repeated, abusive phone calls, which is not only distressing for the target but also for the entire family.

Extortion

Students in primary school are generally not familiar with the term 'extortion'. They usually say that bullies blackmail and threaten you, forcing you to give them your money.

Visual bullying

Visual bullying is also hurtful and degrading for the target. It can take the form of insulting letters passed from student to student or a letter placed in the target's bag or locker. Other forms are graffiti in a public place and e-mails.

Exclusion

Exclusion is when students are deliberately left out of a game or group. For many younger students at primary school this is the most difficult form of bullying to report as it has many subtle expressions. Students will generally describe exclusion as when they are ignored, not allowed to play, made to feel invisible, given the worst job in the group or when the group runs off and hides from them.

Sexual bullying

Sexual bullying consists of obscene drawings and gestures, rude jokes about the target, brushing up against the target, touching when the target does not want to be touched and asking her or him questions of a sexual nature to shame and embarrass.

Racial bullying

Racial bullying can be expressed physically, socially or psychologically when one is labelled negatively as being different from others according to one's race (Besag, 1989). Students at primary school who come from another country often share that they are teased with remarks such as 'your lunch stinks' and 'your skin looks dark and dirty'.

Victim behaviour

It is also important that teachers understand that victim behaviour has many forms. These forms can be broken down into several categories which Besag (1989) has cited in her work. Here are some definitions for easy identification.

Classic victim

One who is not responsible for being bullied (for example, a new student).

Provocative victim

One who provokes and antagonises and then is quick to complain when his or her peers retaliate.

Passive victim

One who is afraid and feels helpless. This student is sometimes on the edge of friendship groups as he or she has difficulty gaining support from peers.

Colluding victim

One who takes on the role of victim to gain acceptance and popularity (for example, the class clown).

False victim

One who complains unnecessarily about his or her peers.

Bully/victim

One who takes on the behaviour of either the bully or the victim, depending on the circumstances.

Purpose of lesson

To introduce students to the meaning and nature of bullying behaviour.

Learning outcome

Students can identify the many forms of bullying behaviour.

Materials required

Activity Sheets 1 and 2a, b (pages 74–6) for each student
butcher paper, felt pens
Role-play sheet, 'Spot the bullying behaviour' (page 73), one copy for each group

Activities

1 Divide the class into six groups, each group consisting of four to six students. Give each group a role-play sheet (see page 73) and allocate one of the six stories for enactment and discussion among themselves before presenting their role-play to the class.

2 At the end of each role-play discuss with the class the following (and record all responses on butcher paper):
   - How might the target have felt while being bullied and after the incident?
   - How might the bully have felt?
   - What were the behaviours of the students doing the bullying?

At the end of the six role-plays students may have thought of other instances of bullying behaviours. Add these to your class list.

Kids at work

Students complete Activity Sheets 1 and 2a,b. Students to copy bullying behaviours from the class list (activity 2 above) for Activity Sheet 1.

Coaching tips

- Be sensitive and selective when grouping students. Avoid placing students who are or have been bullies with those who have been bullied.
- Create a comfortable atmosphere: some children may feel reluctant to share on this issue.
- Keep students focused on the role-plays rather than talking about their own experiences as this may lead to a volatile situation where unresolved conflicts resurface. Do invite them to speak to you privately if they feel the need.
- Leave students with the understanding that: bullying comes in many forms; words and actions are used to make you feel hurt and scared; bullies do this for fun, again and again, sometimes without reason; bullying behaviour is generally disliked.
- Please use your discretion to change the names in the role-plays if you have students in your class with these names.

What kids say

Students provide us with astute comments on their experiences and feelings. Here are some responses that have come out of our workshops in primary schools.

Bullying is when kids:

- swear
- tease
- call you bad names
- start rumours
- say mean stuff about your family
- embarrass you
- steal your stuff and take your money
- put you down
- wreck your things
- write mean notes
- leave you out
- pretend you don't exist
- stalk you
- swear at you in another language
- threaten you and try to get others to join in
- give you the rude finger
- give you greasies
- boss you around
- make you do stuff you don't want to do
- make prank phone calls
- laugh at you
- backstab
- talk behind your back
- gang up on you
- don't let you play
- mimic you
- give you the worst job in the group
- ignore you
- send you nasty e-mails.

Spot the bullying behaviour

Role-play 1

Daniel is playing football with the boys, and every time Daniel has the ball John goes up to him and shoves, punches and kicks him to get the ball. Peter and Howard stand by watching.

Role-play 2

Jan, Amy and Connie are playing. Usually Annette plays with them but the last few weeks Jan has said, 'You can't play with us today'. Annette is confused because she doesn't know what's really happened. She asks Jan why she can't join in. Jan just says, 'Because I'm the boss of this group and I said no'. Jan whispers to Connie and Amy not to let her play or else!

Role-play 3

George, Terry and Vin are having a game on the adventure playground equipment. George says to Terry, 'You're dumb on the monkey bars, you can't even get across in two's. My prep sister can do that. I bet it's because you wear those dumb glasses and those geeky runners. I wouldn't put those on my cat'.

Role-play 4

Chris, Ashleigh and Casey are playing with Gerry. Gerry says of a student they see nearby and on her own, 'She's not playing with us. Look at the colour of her skin. No way! Forget it! People who look like that aren't hanging out with me'.

Role-play 5

During maths Mary writes a mean, rude and untrue note about Susie and passes it around the class. She has done this every day since last week. Mary loves starting rumours.

Role-play 6

Alan is in Grade 3 and is lined up at the canteen ready to buy a packet of chips. Daniel in Grade 5 comes up to him and says, 'Give me your money or else I'll get my two big brothers onto you, so watch out.'

What is Bullying?

Bullying is when someone likes to:

- have power over you
- hurt you with their words and actions
- do the action again and again, sometimes without reason.

Write down the different types of bullying behaviour.

....

....

....

....

....

Bullying behaviour makes me feel:

....

....

....

....

....

....

....

nobody deserves to be bullied

Types of Bullying Behaviour

Bullying can take many forms. Read each of these six examples, then match each person with the type of bullying on activity sheet 2b. Cut and paste into the correct shape.

   Bullying: A Whole-school Approach, ACER Press, © Copyright 2001 Amelia Suckling and Carla Temple

Types of Bullying Behaviour

Match the stories on activity sheet 2a to the correct shape below.

Bullying: A Whole-school Approach, ACER Press, © Copyright 2001 Amelia Suckling and Carla Temple

Why children bully

Fact file

The reasons why bullying occurs are many and complex. The bully may:

- be bullied by others, hence deflects this towards another student
- act in this way for money, possessions and favours
- be confused in his or her notions of leadership (unable to make the distinction between assertive and aggressive behaviour)
- be seeking love and attention
- be lonely and lacking confidence
- be bored
- be seeking revenge
- want to have fun
- have a disruptive family life
- have limited social and interpersonal skills
- be in a school environment that does not take bullying seriously
- feel closer to other members of a group when victimising an outsider.

What the experts say

'It could be that the child has a restricted array of behaviours to choose from due to impoverished experience. Aggression being the simplest and most accessible of behaviours is the one most readily chosen. (Jamieson, cited in Besag, 1989, p. 35)

'A poor self-image, little confidence and feelings of hopelessness can result in some children failing to understand the effect of their behaviour on others.' (Kaplan, cited in Besag, 1989, p. 34)

'Children who bully are less empathetic to the feelings of others (Smith & Thompson, 1991), having little affectional monitoring of their own behaviour.' (Rogers, 1994, p. 101)

Rigby and Slee conducted a survey in primary and secondary schools to find out how students felt when they bullied others. It was alarming to find that over one-third of the boys in primary school and approximately one-quarter of the girls in primary school believed that it stops you from being bullied and close to half of the boys in primary school believed that it gave you a feeling of higher status (Rigby, 1996). Bullying is also about having one's social status elevated within the peer group, or getting pleasure by handing on the aggression that some other bully has given you (Pearce, ch. 9, in Elliot, 1992).

Research also suggests that in some cases bullying is the result of a student getting into the wrong group at the wrong time and engaging in wrong behaviour; it is not necessarily the result of the student having personal problems and difficulties.

Research in Australia has identified bullying as a significant social problem, with one in five children being bullied weekly. Understanding students' motives for bullying and following up with relevant and suitable strategies is vital in reducing the level of bullying in schools.

Purpose of lesson

To reassure students that bullying behaviour exists for many reasons. It does not necessarily mean that there is something wrong with the target or that the target is to blame.

Learning outcome

Students brainstorm and list alternative behaviours to bullying.

Materials required

butcher paper
felt pens
picture, poster or photograph of a group of children (large enough for class display)
Activity Sheet 3 (page 80) for each student

Activities

1 Show the students the picture, poster or photograph of a group of children (who are unknown to the students and completely removed from their environment). Together with the students select any one of the children in the picture as someone whom they are to imagine bullies others.

Through discussion with the students imagine and create a more specific picture of the person. Ask students the following questions:
* What are the details of this person, such as age, personality, interests, family background, strengths, weaknesses?
* Imagine this person bullying someone – what do you see?
* Why do you imagine this person is bullying?
* Do you think this person has ever experienced what he or she is doing to others?

2 Write up students' responses on butcher paper.
* Remind the students that we have a choice about how we behave and that our choices have consequences.
* Ask students if there is another way the imaginary child could behave. Students brainstorm solutions to the problem.

What kids say

Students provide us with astute comments on their experiences and feelings. Here are some responses that have come out of our workshops in primary schools.

Why kids bully:

- they want to show off

- maybe they're bullied at home

- they're jealous of other kids

- they want to be cool and tough

- they're unhappy on the inside

- maybe they used to be bullied by other kids

- they want attention.

- so they don't get bullied by the group

- because their friends make them do it.

Kids at work

The students complete Activity Sheet 3.

Coaching tips

- Steer students away from blaming and punishing (the imaginary child). Lead them to focus on solutions to the problem.
- During the picture chat stay focused on the child in the poster or photograph. Avoid labelling students and personalising incidents that have happened in the classroom or playground.

Some Reasons Why Kids Might Bully

Either by yourself or with a partner write down some positive solutions for each of the problems below in the spaces provided.

lonely

What can kids do when they feel lonely? How can others help?

....
....
....
....

want attention

What other activities can kids do to get attention?

....
....
....
....

Frustrated and ANGRY

What can kids do when they feel frustrated and angry?

....
....
....
....

bored

What can kids do when they are bored?

....
....
....
....

think it's funny

What other ways can kids have fun?

....
....
....
....

Reporting a bullying incident

Fact file

Bullying in schools is covert behaviour that occurs without being witnessed by adults. Students remain quiet because of the stigma in our society about telling tales, fear of reprisal and many other reasons (see below). A major step in reducing bullying is to create a 'telling culture'.

Research conducted by Rigby and Slee through the *Peer Relations Questionnaire* found that over 30 per cent of girls and 40 per cent of boys would not tell if being bullied while others felt unsure as to whether they would tell (Rigby, 1996). This research also indicates that in about half of the cases reported, the bullying situation remained unchanged and in a small percentage of reports the incident became inflamed. These statistics are alarming and illustrate the need for schools to have appropriate procedures in place for reporting followed up with suitable strategies.

It is thus important to reassure those students who choose to report a bullying incident that solutions and resolution will follow. Help the student become clear about the issue, provide strategies, protection if necessary and continued support. You, as the teacher, are placed in a position of trust whereby the student believes that you will take action on his or her behalf in a discreet manner.

Develop mechanisms to ensure that students can report cases of bullying in a safe and private manner. Reassure students that the information they have shared will not cause them to lose status in their peer group. Maintain confidentiality.

In promoting a telling culture it is imperative that teachers guide students to make the distinction between *telling tales* and *responsible reporting* (see page 84 for details).

Why not to tell

All teachers and parents who participate in, respectively, our workshops or information sessions share with us that their students/children do not tell about bullying for many reasons. These are:

- the unwritten code about telling tales
- feeling confused about who to tell and what to say
- feeling ashamed and embarrassed
- believing that teachers will not be able to address the issue
- fearing that the bullying will become intensified
- being afraid that they will be labelled a dobber by their peers
- believing that they deserve it because there is something wrong with them
- having a self-belief that says, 'I'm it, I'm just the kid that everyone picks on'
- being scared of reprisal.

Consequences of bullying

The consequences for the target are many and varied:

- absenteeism
- poor self-esteem
- poor health
- anger
- sadness
- suicide
- inability to form a loving relationship
- suffer a sense of shame, embarrassment and humiliation
- believe what is being said in abusive name-calling.

The consequences for the bully are also diverse and many.

Eron (cited in Marano, 1995) found that adults who as children bullied at school:

- used more government support services
- had higher rates of alcoholism
- displayed more antisocial behaviour
- required more support from mental health agencies.

The damaging consequences of bullying indicate the importance of breaking down the secrecy code as early as possible. Teachers can play a crucial role in building a school ethos that says it's safe to tell. This alone can be the most dynamic and influential prevention tool that schools can adopt.

Purpose of lesson

- To raise students' awareness that everyone in the school plays a dynamic role in developing a 'telling culture'.
- That students understand the importance of asking an adult or their peers for support.

Learning outcomes

- Students can differentiate between responsible reporting and telling tales.
- Students initiate responsible reporting to reduce bullying in the school.
- Students list ways of seeking support from others.

Materials required

Activity Sheets 4 and 5 (pages 85–6)) for each student
butcher paper, felt pens

Activities

1 Discuss the following with your class:
   - What is the difference between responsible reporting and telling tales?
   - What stops students from telling about a bullying incident? (You may wish to list students' responses.)

- What happens if you or someone you know won't tell?
- Who would be the best people to tell?
- What would you do if the person you told did nothing?

2 Explore with students the meanings that can be devised using the acronym DOB. Here are some examples:

DOB   Defend Our Buddies

DOB   Don't Obey Bullies

DOB   Do Object to Bullying

DOB   Dob On Bullies

DOB   Do Our Bit.

3 Brainstorm with the students why it is so important to develop a reporting plan. Help students to explore:

- whom might they tell?
- when is it appropriate to tell?
- how should they tell? (talking to the teacher? taking a friend with them? writing a note? drawing a picture? getting mum or dad to tell?)
- what should they tell?

Students provide us with astute comments on their experiences and feelings. Here are some responses that have come out of our workshops in primary schools.

Why kids don't tell about being bullied:

- because they'll get me
- they'll think I'm a dibber dobber
- friends won't like me any more
- the teacher might not believe me
- I don't know who to tell
- adults won't listen to me
- I might get into trouble myself
- I should be able to solve it myself
- my parents might come up and make a big deal out of it
- it will get worse
- I get so angry I can't think properly
- it's too embarrassing.

Kids at work

Students complete Activity Sheets 4 and 5. For Activity Sheet 4 students may either make up their own DOB messages or copy one from the board.

Coaching tips

- Create an environment in which students will feel safe, secure and confident to tell about a bullying incident.
- If responsible reporting is not encouraged, we sow the seeds of secrecy. Bullying thrives on secrecy and keeps the bully in a powerful position.
- Acknowledge students when they have responsibly reported a bullying incident. This gives the message that their actions do make a difference in building a safe and supportive school environment.
- Making the distinction between *telling tales* and *responsible reporting* is an important one for students. Students will usually say that:

  'Telling tales is when you can really handle the problem yourself but you want to get the other person into trouble. You exaggerate the problem.'

  'Responsible reporting is when the problem is too big for you to handle and you need an adult to help you.'

Just for fun

- You may wish to mount and/or laminate students' DOB posters and reporting plans (Activity Sheets 4 and 5 respectively) and place them in suitable areas around the school.
- Invite guest speakers to the school to talk on bullying in the broader community and strategies for handling it, thus giving students a wider context in which to view the issue.

Responsible Reporting is when you D.O.B.

Write your message for D.O.B. Start each word on the line with the letter given.

D.O.B. means . . .

d ....

o ....

b ....

Now you know the difference between telling tales and responsible reporting, carefully read below. Colour red the squares for telling tales. Colour green the squares for responsible reporting.

Responsible Reporting is when . . .

☐ the problem is serious and you need the support of others.

☐ you feel worried and you can't handle the problem yourself.

this is serious!

Telling Tales is when . . .

☐ it's a small problem.

☐ you may want to get the other person into trouble.

☐ you can really handle the situation yourself.

☐ sometimes it's really untrue.

Don't take the rap ... Report it back

Read what the friend is saying to Target Terry. Then answer the two questions below in the spaces provided.

What's stopping Target Terry from telling?

....

....

....

....

What's wrong Terry? You look worried.

It's nothing really. I can't tell.

But Terry if you don't tell it just gets worse.

Just leave me. I'll be O.K!

What could happen to you if you didn't tell?

....

....

....

....

Ideas to help you go about telling

Colour the ones you would use and write your own ideas on the back of this sheet.

◯ Tell the teacher in private.

◯ Tell a friend, ask him or her to tell the teacher.

◯ Tell mum and dad and ask them to tell the teacher.

◯ Go with a friend to tell the teacher.

◯ Phone Kids Helpline.

◯ Write a letter or draw a picture. Give it to your teacher.

◯ Send your teacher an e-mail.

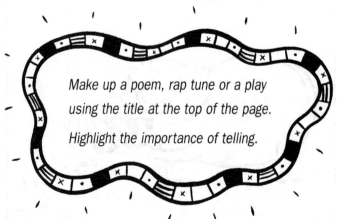

Make up a poem, rap tune or a play using the title at the top of the page.

Highlight the importance of telling.

ACTIVITY SHEET 5: LESSON 3　　　　*Bullying: A Whole-school Approach, ACER Press, © Copyright 2001 Amelia Suckling and Carla Temple*

Locating bullying

Fact file

One may ask, 'Why do schools need to collect data on bullying?' The rationale behind collecting relevant and current data is to:

- raise awareness of the issue in the school community
- quantify the extent of the problem
- locate the hot spots where bullying is occurring most frequently
- give students the message that the issue is being taken seriously
- allow the school community to design appropriate prevention and intervention strategies
- serve as a benchmark to measure the impact of the strategies that have been implemented
- enable staff to work as a team and develop a consistent approach.

When all data have been collected, teachers and other members of staff should consult as to how the results will be discussed with students.

Gathering together relevant information can best be done through using a variety of tools: questionnaires, surveys, photographs and school maps.

Schools need information about:

- how frequently students are bullied
- hot spots for bullying
- whether students have reported being bullied
- how bullying makes students feel
- types of bullying students are experiencing at the school.

Australian studies indicate that students noticed bullying occurring most frequently in the playground during recess and lunch breaks, secondly in the classroom, thirdly on the way home from school and the least on the way to school (Rigby, 1996).

If you have already conducted a bullying audit (survey, questionnaire etc.) in your school, we suggest you keep your results and re-audit later down the track to gauge improvement.

Purpose of lesson

- To locate where bullying occurs.
- To raise awareness of the problem among staff and students.

Learning outcomes

- Students locate areas within the school where bullying occurs.
- Students list possible solutions for improving school safety.

Materials required

Activity Sheets 6 and 7 (pages 90–91) for each student
coloured pencils (red, orange and green)
your own school map (to insert on Activity Sheet 7)
several disposable cameras
letter to parents advising of surveying being administered (see Appendices, page 145)
poster or noticeboard
two envelopes

Activities

1 *Completing a playground questionnaire.* Students will need some explanation as to why they will be completing a questionnaire, for example: 'We would like to find out more about what is happening in our school and we need your support'.

Allow students to be anonymous if they wish and ensure as much privacy as possible. Encourage them to be honest in their responses, assuring them that there are no right or wrong answers (questionnaire is on page 90).

A letter to the parents (provided in the Appendices) advising of a survey being administered is recommended. Apart from the fact that parents would in nearly all cases want to be informed, they may also be able to give extra support.

2 *Drawing an individual school map.* Draw a map of your school (buildings and playground) and paste it onto Activity Sheet 7. Then photocopy the number of activity sheets required so each student has one.

Each child will need three coloured pencils to colour-code their map (red, orange and green). They are to colour in the various areas in the diagram according to their observations of bullying in the school: where it most often happens, happens sometimes, and not at all.

Before taking your class outside to walk through the experience, discuss the meaning of:
high-level bullying   (often)
low-level bullying   (sometimes)
no-bully zone   (none).
Discuss your findings back in the classroom.

3 *Photo safari.* Select a group or groups of five to eight students from your class or you may wish to select your SRC (Student Representative Council). They are to go on a tour, taking with them a member of staff, to photograph places that they like and dislike about their school. Provide each group with a disposable camera. Instruct students on how to use the camera, and encourage each student to take at least one photo. Discussion that occurs among the students during this exercise is important: it may provide the teacher with further knowledge and insight as to what is happening in the school grounds and individual student's responses/attitudes to the situation. This information can be recorded. (Higgins, ch. 7, in Sharp & Smith, 1994a)

4 *Photo board.* Photographs are taken of different locations inside the school buildings and in the playground. Place these on a poster board at eye level. Underneath each photo pin up two envelopes, one marked with a happy face and the other marked with an unhappy face. Ask each student to place a token in the envelope that best describes how they feel about each location. Ask your class to count the tokens for each envelope and discuss your findings. (Sharp, Arora et al., ch. 2, in Sharp & Smith, 1994a)

5 *Random secret ballots.* Ask students to write down on a piece of paper the names of students who are bullying or their three favourite television shows. This avoids the situation of students spying on others to check if they have written anything down. Collect the pieces of paper and see if the names of particular students keep appearing.

Later, interview these students in a non-threatening yet confidential way. You may say something like this:

'We're surprised with the results of the survey. Maybe the results are wrong. It looks like some of your friends are a bit scared of you. That doesn't seem right to us because we know you're a great kid. What do you think? Let us know if we can help you out here.

I know what we will do. Later we will do the survey again and see how those results look. If there is anything we can say or do to let your friends know that they shouldn't be scared of you, let us know.'

This style of survey gives the message that everyone knows what's going on without punishing, shaming or labelling. It also helps break down the anti-dobbing message. (Fuller, 1998.)

Kids at work

Students complete Activity Sheets 6 and 7.

Coaching tip

Before students take part in the activities in this lesson, it is advised that they have a clear understanding of what bullying is (see Lesson 1, pages 69–75).

Just for fun

You may wish to have an anonymous reporting box for your school. Consider first who will be responsible to clear the box and follow up on reports. If there is no follow-up or follow-through, the process is undermined.

 # Investigating Playtime

The teachers would like to help make lunchtime a great time for everyone. Please carefully complete this form.

GRADE: ....   BOY/GIRL (circle)

1 At playtime I like to...

2 My favourite playground place is

....

3 The places I don't like to play in are

....

because..

....

4 What I like best about lunchtime is

....

....

5 At lunchtime I play with

....

....

6 Places in the playground where I have seen bullying are

....

....

....

7 List four things that would make the playground a better place.

....

....

....

....

8 Would you tell someone if you were being bullied? ....

9 Who would you tell?

....

School Map

Be a safety inspector with a classmate and investigate your school for areas where bullying occurs and colour code the different areas below.

Teacher to paste the school map here.

High-level bullying

Colour red on your map.
(It happens every day.)

Low-level bullying

Colour yellow/orange on your map.
(It happens sometimes.)

No bullying

Colour green on your map.
(It never happens.)

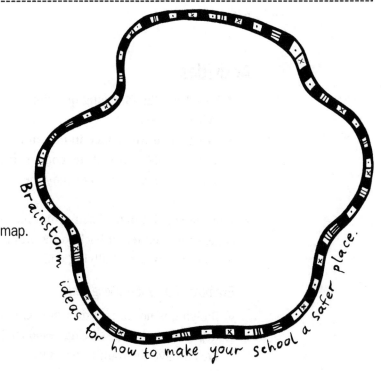

Brainstorm ideas for how to make your school a safer place.

Creating an anti-bullying code

Fact file

An anti-bullying code is not an anti-bullying policy. A code is simply a brief statement on the school's stand on bullying. Students' involvement in writing a code gives them the opportunity to be pro-active. When checking the codes students have written, ensure that they are aligned with the school's current practices.

Purpose of lesson

To post students' graphic representations of their anti-bullying codes as a reminder around the school that will promote a safe-school ethos.

Learning outcome

Students formulate and write an anti-bullying code.

Materials required

Activity Sheet 8 (page 94)
butcher paper
felt pens

Activities

1 Ask students the following questions to open up discussion:
   - What is a code?
   - What could we include in our anti-bullying code?
   - Where could copies of the code be displayed?
   - Why is it important to display these?

2 Work in small groups. Each group has felt pens and butcher paper to design their own code. They then report back to the whole class. The five most suitable points are selected to make a class anti-bullying code.

Example of an anti-bullying code
   - Bullying is not tolerated in our school.
   - Reporting bullying is being responsible.
   - We all have the right to feel safe.

- We all take action to stop bullying.
- Our teachers take bullying seriously.

Kids at work

Students complete Activity Sheet 8, copying the five statements the class has agreed on for their anti-bullying code. Students to present this as carefully as they can.

Coaching tips

- When students are working in their groups, encourage reasoning and conversation for what they select to include in their code.
- Students who talk about bullying and what they can do to prevent it help to promote an anti-bullying ethos.
- Be sensitive and selective when grouping students. Avoid placing students who are or have been bullies with those who have been on the receiving end.

Just for fun

- Place your students' anti-bullying code in appropriate places around the school.
- Select students to read the code at school assembly.
- If other classes have been involved in writing an anti-bullying code, ask the Student Representative Council to select the most suitable points from these to create a school anti-bullying code.
- Send a copy of the code home via the school newsletter for parents to read.

Anti-bullying Code

1. ....
....
....

2. ....
....
....

3. ....
....
....

4. ....
....
....

5. ....
....

The bystander

Fact file

The role of the bystander is crucial to the prevention of bullying. The bystander is more often than not a peer of the bully and/or target of the bullying, and the attitudes and stance of the peer group have a powerful impact on the outcome of the incident. Logic alone would tell us that the majority of the school population falls into the category of bystander. Thus if we can empower the majority to be part of the solution (taking responsible action) and not part of the problem (feeding the power to the bully through inaction or negative actions), we can create a safer and more supportive school environment for all students.

Many bystanders can endorse bullying behaviour quite unconsciously. It can be through lack of action, either by ignoring the bullying situation because it doesn't affect them directly, or inadvertently leaving the target isolated by not inviting him or her to join their friendship group.

Other bystanders are more overt in their endorsement of bullying behaviour: for example, they may laugh and make encouraging comments that spur on the bully.

When conducting our workshops in schools students often say,

- 'But the bully is my friend and if I go to help the target I won't be allowed to play in the group any more and then they might get me.'

- 'It's not my job to do anything. I reckon the teacher should, because what if the bully gets me.'

- 'It's not up to me, she's not in my group, someone else should do it. Anyway, if I say anything, the bully might start picking on me.'

Research by Slee (1996) supports the above. He found that 25.4 per cent of bystanders surveyed would not report an incident because they feared reprisal, 28.3 per cent believed it had nothing to do with them, 30.9 per cent believed that it should be stopped by the teacher, 6.0 per cent believed that it should be stopped by other students and 8.9 per cent thought that the target should handle it for him or herself.

Research on the bystander (Latane & Daly, Latane & Nida, as cited in Sharp & Smith, 1994b) indicates that the higher the number of bystanders witnessing an incident, the less likely it is for someone to take action. This is termed *diffusion of responsibility*.

A tragic example of bystanders' total neglect of responsibility is seen in the murder of James Bulger. It is believed that approximately thirty-five people saw the two ten-year-old boys hurt and forcibly handle James Bulger before he was finally killed. So the sad and obvious question that must be asked is, 'Why didn't anyone stop it?'. Were these witnesses just too busy, did they believe it was none of their business or think that it should be left to someone who would be more capable and confident to deal with it?

Such lack of action had devastating consequences for that little boy, his family and, ultimately, us as a society. It is therefore extremely important for teachers to raise the kudos of being a responsible bystander by publicly praising and acknowledging the efforts and actions of such students. In thus doing we contribute to building a safe school ethos.

To encourage and reward responsible behaviour as a bystander, we have devised the 'Beaut Bystander Certificate' (see Appendices, p. 158), which can be given to students as appropriate.

Purpose of lesson

- To promote a shared understanding of respect, fairness and responsibility.
- To raise students' awareness that the bystanders' actions are part of either the solution or the problem.
- To encourage students to be responsible bystanders and thus contribute to building a safe and supportive environment.

Learning outcome

Students identify behaviours of the bystander that encourage and that discourage bullying.

Materials required

Activity Sheet 9 (page 100)
Role-play sheet, 'What do I do now?' (page 99), one copy for each group
Poster 1 (Appendices, page 151), enlarged

Activities

1 Discuss with the students the meaning of the word *bystander*. There are various types of bystanders (as mentioned in the Fact File):
   - one who does nothing and ignores the situation
   - one who behaves negatively and spurs on the bully
   - one who takes responsible action.

2 Ask the students what stops a bystander from taking action in our school. Here are some examples of what students are saying in the schools we visit: 'I'm too scared'; 'they'll call me a dobber'; 'they won't be my friend'; 'they'll get me next time'; 'why should I, I'm glad it's not me'; 'someone else should tell'; 'I could get hurt'; 'the teacher should deal with it'.

3 Ask the students what are the consequences when the bystander doesn't take action. Here are some sample answers:
   - 'The bullies get away with it.'
   - 'The bully may decide to target others because no one is stopping him or her.'
   - 'Other students may copy the bullying behaviour, believing it is acceptable.'
   - 'It gives the message to the target that he or she deserves it.'
   - 'The target continues to feel scared and isolated.'

4 Discuss with the students how bystanders can make the bullying worse.

5 Ask and discuss with the class what actions a bystander can take. Your students may come up with a list similar to those given below. List your students' responses.

Negative reactions	Positive actions
laugh	tell others to leave the scene
giggle	tell an adult immediately
say nothing	tell the student who is bullying to stop it
join the bullying	ask the target to join in your game
stare	go with the target to the teacher
point	tell others that bullying is uncool
tell others it's fun to watch	ask the target if they are okay
do nothing: 'glad it's not me'	stand near the target
	don't smile or join in

Show students the enlarged Poster 1. Add any other comments from the discussion to the poster.

6 Ask students, which actions encourage bullying? which actions discourage bullying? (Mark these on your list compiled in question 5.)

7 Divide the class into five groups, each group consisting of four to six students. Each group is given one of the five role-plays 'What do I do now?' on page 99 to present to the class. Display Poster 1 to assist students in their responses.

The role-plays will help students gain a feeling of what it is like to be a bully, a bystander and a target in a bullying situation. At the end of each role-play encourage the students to share their individual experiences of their role.

What kids say

Students provide us with astute comments on their experiences and feelings. Here are some responses that have come out of our workshops in primary schools.

Often students will refer to the bystanders who are colluding with the bully as the bully's:

- backup team
- slaves
- sheep
- alibi
- sidekicks
- gang
- followers
- wannabees
- trainees
- mob
- shadows
- tag-alongs.

One Year 3 student shared with us:

'... that if you say or do something to stop the bullying as a bystander, you drain the bully's power away.'

Kids at work

Students complete Activity Sheet 9 (page 100).

Coaching tips

Under no circumstances should we expect children to put themselves in a position of breaking up fights or heated arguments where they can be hurt.

What do I do now?

Role-play 1

A group of students in the playground takes another student's basketball and refuses to give it back to him. The responsible bystanders say and do …

Role-play 2

A student lines up at the canteen to buy lunch. An older student comes up and says, 'Give me your lunch money or else I'll get you'. The responsible bystanders say and do …

Role-play 3

Josie starts a rumour about Annie. Josie whispers the rumour to Sue who whispers the message around the class. Annie can see what is going on but is too afraid to say anything. The responsible bystanders say and do …

Role-play 4

A group of students laugh as they trip over a younger student called Jim again and again. Jim tells them to stop it but they gather around him and continue laughing at him and putting him down. Jim feels humiliated, embarrassed and frightened. The responsible bystanders say and do …

Role-play 5

A group of students plays a game of soccer. Paul stares and says to Bill, 'You can't play with us, you're hopeless at soccer. Just because we let you play yesterday doesn't mean we will let you play today'. Paul tries to get the others in his group to back him up. The responsible bystanders say and do …

Bystanders

Carefully read the think bubbles.
Colour red the thoughts that stop bystanders taking action.
On the back of this sheet draw yourself being a responsible bystander.

Bystander's Action: Tick what you would do

		Yes	No	Unsure
1	walk away			
2	stare			
3	say nothing and be relieved it's not me			
4	join in with the bully			
5	laugh, think it's funny			
6	tell an adult			
7	stand near the target for support			
8	tell others it's fun to watch			
9	take the target away			
10	go with the target to tell an adult			
11	tell the others you don't like what the bully is doing			
12	ask the target to join your game			
13	tell the bully to stop it			

How might the target feel when bystanders do nothing or say things to encourage the bullying?

....

....

How might the target feel when bystanders take responsible action?

....

....

   Bullying: A Whole-school Approach, ACER Press, © Copyright 2001 Amelia Suckling and Carla Temple

LESSON 7

The bystander's code

Purpose of lesson

To write and graphically represent a students' bystander's code; to then place it in strategic spots around the school, promoting a school ethos that says taking action is being responsible.

Learning outcome

Students formulate and write a bystander's code.

Materials required

Activity Sheet 10 (page 103) for each student
butcher paper
felt pens
lightweight cardboard to mount students' work (optional)

Activities

1   *Warm-up game: Take a Stand on Ten*
    Read out to the class the ten statements below to which they can respond *yes* or *no*.
    - I bully others so I don't become a target!
    - Reporting a bullying incident is being responsible!
    - I can take action by going with the target to tell a teacher!
    - It is only the teacher's job to deal with bullying!
    - If I see physical bullying I should go and break it up by standing between the bully and the target!
    - I tell the child who is bullying the target to stop it!
    - I choose to use my words to help the target. I say, 'Are you okay, do you want to join our game?'
    - I tell others that bullying is cool as long as they leave me alone!
    - When bullying occurs I tell others to hang around and watch!
    - I stand around and watch the bullying behaviour and the target at lunchtime for fun!

2   Discuss with the students the following:
    - What is a code?
    - What could we include in our bystander's code?

101

- Where could we display copies of the bystander's code?
- Why is it important to display these?

3 Students work in small groups. Each group has felt pens and butcher paper to design their own bystander's code. Students discuss and brainstorm ideas for the code; they can also select from the list of bystander's actions written up in the previous lesson.

When all groups have finalised among themselves their selection of points for the code, each group reports back to the class. The most suitable points overall are then selected to make a class bystander's code.

Below is a sample of students' ideas for a bystander's code:

Bystander's code

- Don't join in.
- Don't smile to show that you agree with the bully's behaviour.
- Tell others you don't like the bullying behaviour.
- Call a teacher for help immediately.
- Go with the target to tell the teacher.
- Show care for the target by standing near him or her.
- Ask the bullied student to join your game.
- Ask the student if she or he feels okay.
- Distract the student who is bullying.

Kids at work

Students copy the class bystander's code onto Activity Sheet 10, presenting it colourfully.

Coaching tip

When students are working in their groups, encourage reasoning and conversation for what they have selected as appropriate for a bystander's code and where these ideas can be displayed. When teachers provide students with the opportunity both formally and informally to discuss responsible and fair behaviour, a stronger social conscience develops, which influences the ethos of the school.

Just for fun

Place your students' bystander's code in strategic spots around the school, select students to read it at school assembly and send a copy home via the school newsletter for parents to read.

Bystander's Code

1. ....

2. ....

3. ....

4. ....

5. ....

6. ....

Your responsible actions can help STOP Bullying.

Anti-bullying slogans

Fact file

We can build and promote the ethos of a 'telling school' (see page 50) by continuing to raise the school community's awareness of bullying. Slogans and posters can be fun, effective and non-threatening if used wisely. The policies and practices throughout the school should support the slogans students design.

Purpose of lesson

To display around the school students' graphic representations of anti-bullying slogans as a reminder of the school's stand on building and maintaining a safe and supportive environment for the school community.

Learning outcome

Students design and display their graphic representations of anti-bullying slogans for placement around the school.

Materials required

Activity Sheet 11 (page 106) for each student
felt pens

Activities

1 Brainstorm with your students possible slogans that could be used to post around the school. Encourage students to use positive language. Some examples are:
   - fair is fun for everyone
   - we all have the right to feel safe and be safe
   - bullying is taken seriously in our school
   - Cool Dudes Report Bullying
   - co-operation is cool.

2 Students form small groups of between five and seven to discuss the slogans they are going to use.

Kids at work

Students write in their slogans on their individual Activity Sheets and fill out the page with illustration and/or a decorative design.

Just for fun

- The student activity sheets can be enlarged to A3 size, mounted onto coloured cardboard and then laminated to make mini-posters. These can be posted around the school.
- Have a poster competition and award prizes to students who best capture the ethos of a safe and supportive school. Approach your local businesses to donate prizes. To send the message further out into the community, invite local media to write a story on the students' activities, which will promote the school's pro-active stand on preventing bullying.

Anti-bullying Slogans

Buddies

Fact file

'Studies show that task performance among delinquent adolescents was at its highest when they were reinforced by their peers rather than an adult' (Brown, Reschly & Sabers, cited in Rogers, 1998, p. 255). Teachers and students will tell us that obvious and deliberate action is needed to encourage the target to talk about his or her bullying experience. If we can set structures in place such as a buddy for the target, we can help create a healthy relationship between peers.

The purpose of a buddy is to offer friendship in a variety of ways, to offer protection if and when needed, and model ways of joining a group, of knowing how to maintain friends and how to cope with conflict.

Buddies need to be selected with care and sensitivity. Students should not feel obliged to take on this role, rather volunteer under the guidance and judgment of the teacher. So that the role of the buddy does not become burdensome, regular changes would be beneficial. The teacher needs to keep in mind that the goals of a buddy system are to provide protection if necessary, give an experience of friendship and model coping strategies.

To encourage and reward a buddy for the support and friendship he or she has given, we have devised the 'Great Mate Certificate' (Appendices, page 159), which can be given to students as appropriate.

Purpose of lesson

To train buddies in the necessary skills to support children who are targets of bullying.

Learning outcome

Students discuss and list the positive characteristics of a supportive buddy.

Materials required

Activity Sheet 12 (page 109) for those students selected to be buddies
felt pens
butcher paper

Activities

1   Discuss the following with your students and what it means to be and to have a buddy.
    - What is a buddy?
    - Why is a buddy important for some students?
    - What makes a good buddy?
    - What are some things a buddy can do? (brainstorm)

2   Read together the list of roles a buddy can play on Activity Sheet 12 and discuss further suggestions. When developing a role description for a buddy, your students' suggestions may look something like this:
    - Share play lunch.
    - Meet your buddy at the school gate and walk her or him to the classroom.
    - During recess and lunchtime spend some time with your buddy (share a book, a game, play the computer, have a chat).
    - For ease of finding your buddy in the playground, decide where you will meet each other.
    - Walk your buddy to the toilet if necessary.
    - Invite your buddy to join in your games.
    - Write a friendly note to encourage your buddy.
    - Give tips when tricky problems come up.
    - Model positive verbal and body language.

Kids at work

Students complete Activity Sheet 12.

Coaching tips

- You may wish to run this session with a selected group of students, possibly out of class time.
- Buddies can be from the same class, or from a different class or level.
- Provide regular feedback chats so that you can evaluate, acknowledge and offer support for the buddy.
- Be attentive to the fact that at some point the buddy may wish to discontinue in the role. If necessary, re-appoint another buddy for the bullied student.
- A buddy's role is a short-term measure to support a variety of strategies (prevention and intervention) that are implemented throughout the entire school.

Being a Buddy is Beaut

Beaut Buddies can:

- share playlunch.
- meet their buddies at the school gate and walk them into class.
- spend time with their buddies at recess.
- invite their buddies to join in their games.
- model positive body language.
- give tips when their buddies are having trouble.
- help their buddies keep their cool.
- phone or e-mail their buddies at home as a form of friendship.

Add your own suggestions:

....

....

In the space below write what you can say to your buddy.

Draw a picture on the back of this sheet of yourself supporting your buddy.

A Beaut Buddy can say ...

I like the way you ....

....

You're getting better at ....

....

It's OK. Don't react ....

....

Beaut Buddy's Oath

I promise to be responsible and reliable.

I promise to be a positive role-model.

★

DATE TO START ....

DATE TO FINISH ....

MY BUDDY IS ....

SIGNATURE ....

LESSON 10

Staying in Neutral Zone

Fact file

These two definitions give an excellent idea of the reclaiming power of assertiveness.

> 'Assertiveness is aimed at standing up for one's own rights in such a way that the rights of other people are not violated.' (Back & Back, 1991, cited in Randall, 1996, p. 1)

> 'Assertiveness is also about regaining control and empowerment to take back whatever valuable feelings of confidence, beliefs in oneself and positive self-constructs that faulty socialisation processes and bullying behaviour have taken away.' (Randall, 1996, p. 135)

Students need to be taught as early as possible how to assert themselves effectively. If students are able to express their feelings and needs while being respectful of others, they will be neither bully nor victim.

When students are encouraged to investigate and trust their inner world (thoughts, feelings and attitudes) and have this supported with a repertoire of strategies for assertiveness, they will be more able to handle peer pressure.

Learning how to be assertive in a variety of situations is a necessary life-skill that students can apply not only when they are threatened but in many everyday circumstances; conflict is a part of everyday life. Empowering students with the skills to understand the consequences and repercussions of their behaviour and the belief that they have a *choice* about this is a prerequisite for adulthood.

To avoid becoming the target of bullying, students need to be made aware of behaviour (in actions, tone of voice, words and body language) that may make them vulnerable. Reactions that are either aggressive or passive may equally make students vulnerable to being bullied. When students behave in an aggressive and/or passive manner they may inadvertently reward or satisfy the bullies. Hence the target is at risk of further victimisation.

The following four lessons aim to move students out of reactive behaviour into another way of operating that is known as *Neutral Zone.* This zone describes the mind space where students find themselves when they choose not to react to a situation, verbally or in action, with either aggression or passivity. One way to encourage students to build resilience and inner strength and stay in Neutral Zone, is to ask them to visualise a clear plastic safety shield surrounding and protecting them. When nasty, mean words are directed to them, they bounce back to where they came from.

It is imperative that students are able to make clear distinctions between the terminologies *passive, aggressive* and *assertive* so they can then gauge their own and others' behaviour.

Purpose of lesson

- To make students aware of the different ways of relating to others (passive, aggressive and assertive) and the consequences of each behaviour.

110

STANDING FIRM IN NEUTRAL ZONE		
PASSIVE	ASSERTIVE	AGGRESSIVE
Doing nothing and hoping to get what you want.	*Saying what you think, feel and want in a calm and confident way.*	*Getting your own way at all costs*
BEHAVIOURS looking weak whingeing giving in sulking crying	**BEHAVIOURS** no put-downs saying what you want calm, clear voice appearing confident (even when you feel scared) eye contact standing still	**BEHAVIOURS** shouting fighting arguing shaming blaming
CONSEQUENCES lowered self-confidence likelihood of provocation to continue makes one an easy target	**CONSEQUENCES** gives message of being in control of oneself by not overreacting	**CONSEQUENCES** inflames the conflict/bullying
REACTiON	NO REACTION	REACTiON

Diagram 7 Standing firm in Neutral Zone.

- To teach students the meaning and effectiveness of staying in Neutral Zone in a situation of conflict.
- To teach students to visualise a safety shield in threatening and confronting situations.

Learning outcomes

- Students can identify aggressive, passive and assertive behaviours.
- Students can recognise the consequences of assertive, aggressive and passive behaviours.

Materials required

Posters 2, 3 and 4 (Appendices, pages 152–4), each to be enlarged for classroom discussion
Operating in Neutral Zone: Chris and Lee stories (page 113)
Activity Sheets 13 and 14 (pages 114–15), one for each student
butcher paper
felt pens

Activities

1 Present students with Posters 2, 3 and 4 in conjunction with reading them the Chris and Lee stories. Read Story 1: Passive response and write down the students' responses to the story, asking questions such as:
- How did Lee feel?
- What did Lee do in this story to encourage Chris? (Answers might include: sulk, whinge, use a small voice, weak body language, no eye contact, put herself down, give in.)
- How did Lee's behaviour (reaction) make Chris feel? (Possible answers could include: powerful, that she wants to show off, dominant.)

2 Read Story 2: Assertive response and write down the students' responses to the story, asking questions such as:
- How did Lee behave? (Students list the behaviours.)
- Is the bullying more likely to continue in Story 1 or 2? Why?

3 Read Story 3: Aggressive response and write down the students' responses to the story, asking questions such as:
- How did Lee feel?
- What did Lee do in Story 3 that encouraged Chris? (yell, argue, blame, put Chris down)

4 Draw students' attention to the terms *passive, aggressive* and *assertive* and discuss with them the meaning of each.

5 Discuss with the students why the assertive behaviour worked. (Lee chose not to react and stayed in Neutral Zone. Some indicators of this were that Lee: had eye contact; stood still; didn't use put-downs; spoke in a clear, calm voice; appeared confident; said what she wanted.) Ask students to talk about the times when it helps to stay in Neutral Zone.

6 Together with the students discuss each of the skills as listed in 5 above that enabled Lee to be assertive. Ask students to stand and demonstrate.

Kids at work

Students complete Activity Sheets 13 and 14. For Activity Sheet 14 show students the enlarged Posters 2, 3 and 4. Students will need to select and copy the appropriate words for each of the behaviours passive, aggressive and assertive.

Coaching tip

Many students cannot make the distinction between aggressive and assertive behaviour. It is important that the differences are well defined and explored so that students can see, hear, feel and almost taste the sometimes subtle but big differences between these two behaviours.

Just for fun

Select and tape snippets of popular television programs that illustrate aggressive, assertive and passive responses. Show these to the students and discuss with them the body language and verbal language used.

Operating in Neutral Zone: Chris and Lee stories

Story 1 Passive response

Chris and her group stand over Lee. Chris says, 'You better give me your pens, baby face.' Lee knows this group has a reputation for getting into trouble and has had enough of Chris's constant threats. Lee says in a sulky, whingeing voice, 'Oh stop it, that's not fair, they're mine,' as she looks to the ground.

Chris yells back in a loud angry voice, 'Are you going to give me the pens or not?'.

Lee answers in an unsure, small voice, 'I think so'. Chris yells back, 'If you know what's good for you, you'll do as I say or else' as she snatches the pens from Lee's hand.

Lee bursts into tears and Chris and her group laugh at Lee, wondering what they will take from her tomorrow. Lee feels embarrassed that she gave in so easily.

Story 2 Assertive response

Chris and her group stand over Lee. Chris says in a loud, threatening voice, 'Give me your new gold pens to keep, baby face'. Lee knows this group has a bad reputation and she feels her stomach tighten. Lee reminds herself to look confident no matter how she feels. She makes a picture in her mind of a clear plastic dome surrounding and protecting her. She calls this her safety shield. Lee looks Chris in the eye and says in a calm, clear voice, 'No, these gold pens are mine'.

Chris gets angry and annoyed and speaks in a louder voice saying, 'Give me those gold pens, you loser'. Lee keeps her cool. She stands firm without fidgeting and says to Chris, 'These pens are not for anyone else'. Chris does not like it when the people she targets do not react. She makes a mean face at Lee and says, 'You must be an idiot, just watch out'. Lee calmly answers, 'Maybe' and walks away.

Chris's group snigger, saying, 'Who does she think she is?'. Lee understands that it's not worth having the last word. She pretends not to hear their sniggers and chooses not to react.

Story 3 Aggressive response

Chris and her group stand over Lee and Chris says, 'Give me your new gold pens, baby face, or you'll be sorry'. Chris and her group have been at Lee again and again. Lee says in an angry voice, 'No way, get your own, you cheapskate. You probably haven't got enough money so you have to take mine'.

Chris yells back in a threatening voice, 'Give me those gold pens now or there will be trouble'. Lee shoves Chris in the shoulder yelling, 'Get lost loser'. Chris yells louder, demanding that Lee better do exactly what she says and snatches the pens. Lee grabs the pens back, tearing the packet, yelling to Chris that she's a hopeless loser.

Chris and her group enjoy seeing Lee lose control, it makes them feel powerful. During the argument Lee drops the pens and a student passing by accidentally stands on them.

Safety Shield

Draw yourself inside your Safety Shield.

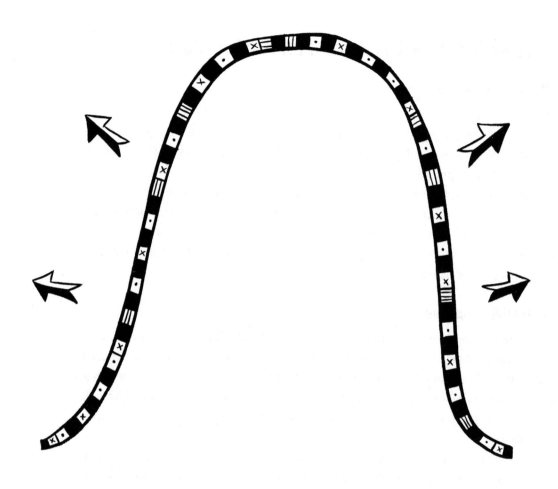

I am in charge of my behaviour.
*Here I am standing firm in **NEUTRAL ZONE**.*

My Safety Shield helps me ....

....

It makes me feel ....

....

Passive, Assertive, Aggressive

Write down examples of passive, assertive and aggressive behaviour in the spaces provided.
Draw a picture for each in the boxes provided below.

Passive

....
....
....
....
....
....
....

Assertive

....
....
....
....
....
....

Aggressive

....
....
....
....
....
....

Stand Firm in NEUTRAL ZONE

Looking Weak

Looking Assertive

Looking Aggressive

Say 'no' like you mean it

Fact file

Saying 'no' like you mean it is much more difficult than it sounds. Students need to know that they have the right to say 'no'. It is crucial that they know how to use their body language and tone of voice appropriately. Children not only have to work out how to say 'no' but when they have the right to say 'no'.

Purpose of lesson

- To teach students the rules for saying 'no'.
- To teach students the benefits of operating from the position of Neutral Zone.

Learning outcomes

- Students identify the three types of body language: passive, aggressive and assertive.
- Students demonstrate assertive body language when saying 'no' in Neutral Zone.

Materials required

Posters 2, 3 and 4 (Appendices, pages 152–4), each to be enlarged for classroom discussion
Role-play sheet, 'Ways of saying no' (page 118) for each student (to be used in conjunction with Activity Sheet 15)
Activity Sheet 15 (page 119) for each student
scissors and paste

Activities

1 Discuss and act out the body language of passive, aggressive and assertive behaviours with the students, consolidating what they have learnt in the previous lesson.

2 Introduce the rules for saying 'no':
- look the person in the eye
- don't mumble, fidget, giggle, sulk
- confident body language
- stay cool and calm in Neutral Zone
- give reasons when necessary

- no put-downs
- don't argue back.

3 Discuss and act out with students ways of saying 'no', using the following examples:
- 'No, I don't lend my bike.'
- 'No, I will not give you my money.'
- 'No, I won't steal Tom's pen to be part of your group.'

4 Divide the class into six groups, each group consisting of five to six students. Each group is given one of the six role-plays, 'Ways of saying no' to act out and present to the class. Display Posters 2, 3 and 4 to assist the students' discussion on how each story illustrates a particular type of behaviour. Ask students to categorise the behaviour of each as either passive, aggressive or assertive and to notice what behaviour is effective and what isn't.

Kids at work

Students complete Activity Sheet 15, selecting one story each from the role-play sheet for passive, aggressive and assertive behaviour. Then cut them out and paste each story onto the Activity Sheet in the appropriate box.

Coaching tips

- Model the three ways of saying 'no' (passive, assertive, aggressive) to help students see clearly the differences between them.
- Invite students to investigate how they feel when they say 'no' in Neutral Zone.
- Be sensitive in grouping your students for the role-plays. Creating positive dynamics within your class is crucial. Place vulnerable and supportive students together and aggressive students with those who are resilient.
- Remind students to use their safety shield.

Just for fun

- Students role-play a variety of responses using puppets or masks.
- When a conflict has occurred among students, ask those involved to replay the situation, steering students by asking:
- Is there another way you could do that?
- Is there a better way to use your words?
- What happens when you change your tone and body language?
  Your questioning needs to direct students to resolve conflicts firmly and fairly.
- Make a *People Power Poster*. In small groups cut out pictures from old magazines of people expressing a range of body language and paste them onto large sheets of paper. Categorise the body language into passive, aggressive or assertive. Students place a tick beside the figures that have assertive body language.

Ways of saying no

Story 1

Joe has a new calculator. Vin and his mates want to use it when Joe is using it. Vin has a reputation for putting people down to get what he wants. Vin says to Joe in a threatening voice, 'You better give me your calculator or else'. Joe yells back, 'Get lost you idiot, it's mine. Go and buy your own, loser'. Their friends tell both of them to calm down. Vin becomes more aggressive because he wants to get his own way and look powerful in front of his group. Vin demands the calculator again and Joe yells back while Vin snatches the calculator. Vin enjoys making Joe lose control.

Story 2

Bill and his group yell at John, demanding his ball. 'Give it to me, give it to me or else you're in big trouble'. John whispers 'no' under his tears, mumbling and fidgeting. Bill runs off with the ball.

Story 3

Mary and Tom keep arguing about who will take home the shared project they had finished. Tom says, 'I should take it because I did most of the work'. Mary yells at Tom, 'That's not true, I did most of the work, I'm taking it home'. She continues yelling at Tom and becomes so angry that she kicks his bag. Tom goes to grab the project and it tears. Their friends remind them to be calm and stay in Neutral Zone.

Story 4

Dylan and his group want Shannon's lemon cake because he has finished his own lunch and is still hungry. Shannon looks Dylan in the eye and says in a confident voice, 'No, this is my lunch and I am hungry too'. Dylan walks away feeling hungry.

Story 5

Jackie and her friends start annoying Sarah, encouraging her to do something she does not think is fair. Sarah says clearly and calmly, 'No, I can't do that, she's my friend'. She looks Jackie in the eye as she says this. Sarah stands tall, looks cool and calm but on the inside she feels a bit scared.

Story 6

John and his gang say to Tom, 'Give me your lunch money now or I'll tell everyone about your brother'. Tom looks down at his shoes, fidgeting and sulking as he mumbles, 'No, that's my money to spend'. John easily snatches the money out of Tom's hand, runs off and spends it. John thinks, 'Hey that was easy. I'll try the same again tomorrow'.

Rules for Saying 'No'

DO

Stand firm
give eye contact
say what you want
Speak in a clear voice
look confident (even if you're scared)

DON'T

use put-downs
shout
mumble, fidget, giggle
sulk
whinge
whisper
argue back

Paste in a story under each heading.

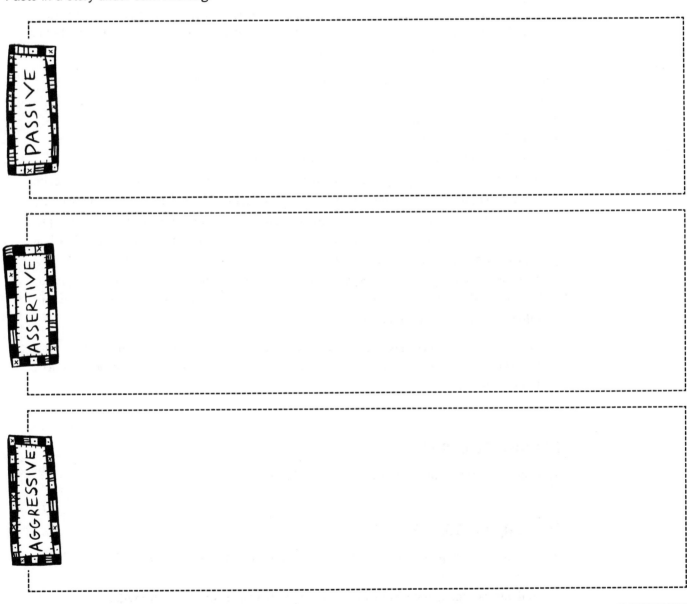

PASSIVE

ASSERTIVE

AGGRESSIVE

With a partner write/draw your own ASSERTIVE script for saying NO. Present this to the class.

Bullying: A Whole-school Approach, ACER Press, © Copyright 2001 Amelia Suckling and Carla Temple

Using 'I' messages

Fact file

'An I-Message is authentic, honest and congruent – reflecting the actual nature and strength of your thoughts and feelings. It is a clear message, understandable and to the point, not masked in indirect or vague language.' (Gordon, 1988, p. 38)

An 'I' message has specific features. These include that the speaker:

- starts his or her message with 'I'
- describes how he or she feels
- states his or her needs
- does not use language that puts down someone else.

An 'I' message thus requires the student to state clearly what he or she wants in a calm and direct manner without demeaning others. Being assertive means taking responsibility for your feelings, thoughts and words without blaming others (Berne, 1996). For example, the statement, 'You better shut your mouth or I'll kick you' becomes, 'I don't like it when you speak to me like that. I want you to stop'.

An 'I' message can be used in response to teasing, name-calling and mild, physical provocation. The student needs to operate from Neutral Zone, creating non-reactionary behaviour that does not escalate the situation.

'You-Messages are statements, judgments, guesses, evaluations, labels and the like of other people and things. You-Messages generally create hurt feelings, defensiveness and resistance to others.' (Gordon, 1988, p. 39)

Purpose of lesson

That students understand the features of an 'I' message.

Learning outcomes

- Students can express themselves with appropriate 'I' messages as a form of being assertive.
- Students can make the distinction between 'I' messages and 'you' messages.

Materials required

Activity Sheet 16 (page 123) for each student
Posters 2, 3 and 4 (Appendices, pages 152–4), enlarged for classroom discussion
'you' messages written on individual cards (see activity 3)

Activities

1 Display the enlarged Posters 2, 3 and 4 to the class and then explore how body language is affected when you use 'I' messages and 'you' messages and which of the statements might relate to which poster. The students can then stand up and physically act out the following two statements:

'You always push me around. You're mean.'
'I don't like it when I'm pushed around.'

You can then model these two statements to the class.

2 Outline the features of an 'I' message to the class.

3 Students move into small groups of about four or five in each. Give each group one card with a 'you' message (see messages below) and ask them to discuss and change it into an 'I' message. Each group reports back, reading first the 'you' message followed by the 'I' message. The class observes the difference in tone, pitch and body language between the two messages as they are being read. (Likely 'I'-message responses are given in italics below.)

- 'You can't make me. Do it yourself lazybones.'
  'I don't want to do that now. I want to finish my game'.

- 'You always blame me when your pens go missing.'
  'I feel like a thief when you say that. I didn't take your pens, I have my own.'

- 'You leave me out all the time, you hate me, you're mean.'
  'I don't have anyone to play with. I'd like to join your game.'

- 'You always push me when we line up. It's not fair.'
  'I feel angry when you stand on my feet. I want you to leave me alone.'

- 'You always say I'm hopeless at sport. You're hopeless yourself.'
  'I feel embarrassed when you say that. I'm not that interested in sport. Don't say that again.'

- 'You'll be sorry for putting your stuff on my hook. Watch out.'
  'I feel angry when you take my hook. This is the hook I've been given, you'll have to find your own.'

4 If teasing and put-downs persist, students need to be encouraged to ask for support. Introduce the Four Steps and Tell technique. An example is given here.
   a 'I don't like it when you swear at me. Stop it.'
   b Repeat step a.
   c 'I will tell the teacher if you do not stop swearing at me. I want you to stop it.'
   d 'I'm going to tell the teacher.'

   - Role-play these steps with selected students to the class.
   - Then rehearse the steps with the entire class, speaking the lines in unison, and checking the tone of voice students use.
   - Finally, students rehearse in pairs, checking that tone of voice and body language do not escalate the situation.

Kids at work

Students complete Activity Sheet 16.

Coaching tips

Help students to notice the difference in body language and tone of voice when they use 'I' messages to when they use 'you' messages.

Just for fun

- Ask students to listen for 'I' messages used by parents, teachers and friends.
- Ask students to listen for 'I' messages when watching their favourite television programs.
- *'I'-message/'you'-message poster* Students paste their 'I'-message/'you'-message cards from this lesson onto a class poster, illustrating the likely consequences of using an 'I' message and also using a 'you' message.

Help Max to be an 'I'-Message Master

Read the think bubbles below.
Colour RED the 'you' messages. Colour GREEN the 'I' messages.

When Max uses 'I' messages it helps him stay in charge of his feelings and behaviour.

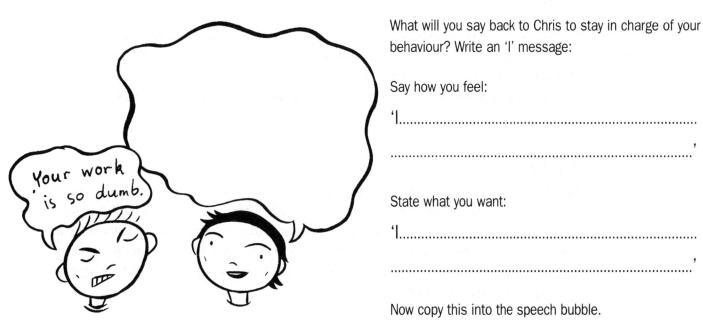

What will you say back to Chris to stay in charge of your behaviour? Write an 'I' message:

Say how you feel:

'I..
....,'

State what you want:

'I..
....,'

Now copy this into the speech bubble.

   Bullying: A Whole-school Approach, ACER Press, © Copyright 2001 Amelia Suckling and Carla Temple

Using Robot Voice and Fogging

Fact file

Robot Voice

It can be difficult for a child (and also an adult) to confront a barrage of threatening statements. One way of staying in control of the situation is to remain in Neutral Zone (pages 110–13) and continue repeating the same assertive statement until the bully is bored because he or she is not getting the desired reactionary response.

In the texts this technique is referred to as 'Broken Record' (Sharp, Cowie & Smith, ch. 5, in Sharp & Smith, 1994a). Our experience when conducting workshops in schools indicates that many students have no understanding of what a record is, so we renamed the strategy 'Robot Voice'. Students understand that when a robot speaks, its tone of voice and the words it uses remain unchanged; its language is unemotional and non-reactionary.

In this strategy for assertiveness the target responds by repeating the same 'I' message with the same tone of voice, words and body language. Here is an example:

| Student 1: | Give me your game. |
| Student 2: | *No, I don't lend this game.* |

| Student 1: | Give me your game, I lent you my pens last week. |
| Student 2: | *Thanks for your pens but I don't lend this game.* |

| Student 1: | Give me your game or else you'll be sorry. |
| Student 2: | *No, I don't lend this game.* |

Students need to be reminded that it is normal to feel scared and threatened but to give the message that they are in control. They also need to keep in mind that if the threats continue, they must 'walk away' and tell an adult.

The repetitious words, tone and body language used enable the target to stay in Neutral Zone.

Fogging

Fogging (Sharp & Smith, 1994a) is a technique that may be used by the target when he or she is being teased and put down. The target responds to each taunt or name with a neutral statement. During our workshops students often say, 'You just agree with the bully like you don't care about what they are saying'. By thus responding the situation does not become inflamed. The bully soon becomes bored because the target is not reacting in the way that was expected. Here's an example of Fogging.

Student 1:	You look silly.
Student 2:	*Maybe.*
Student 1:	Your haircut is so dumb.
Student 2:	*You might think so.*
Student 1:	I bet the butcher cut it, not the hairdresser.
Student 2:	*Shrugs shoulders.*
Student 1:	Anyway, your haircut makes you look like a three-year-old.
Student 2:	*Possibly.*
Student 1:	And if you think you're going to be in our group, forget it.
Student 2:	*So.*

Safety shield

Students are encouraged to visualise themselves inside their own personal safety shield (page 110). Any negative put-downs are deflected, and the imagery helps slow down possible reactions. Students can use this in conjunction with all the strategies for assertiveness.

These strategies for assertiveness may not necessarily take away students' feelings of fear or anger when threatened. What they can do is help give students the impression that they are in charge and in control of their behaviour.

Purpose of lesson

To extend students' repertoire of strategies for assertiveness using Fogging and Robot Voice, supported by visualising their own safety shield.

Learning outcome

Students apply and practise the strategies of Robot Voice and Fogging, staying in Neutral Zone.

Materials required

Stories illustrating Fogging and Robot Voice (page 127)
Activity Sheet 17 (page 128) for each student
Posters 2, 3, 4 and 5 (Appendices, pages 152–5), enlarged

Activities

1 Explain the meaning of Fogging to students.
(Fogging means responding to teasing and name-calling with neutral words that don't give off a reaction. Words like *maybe, could be, so, possibly, if you think so,* said in a cool, calm, confident way and shrugging one's shoulders.)

2 Read Story 1: Sue and Julie (page 127) to the class. Ask students:
• How would you describe Sue's body language?

- How might Sue be feeling?
- Did Sue stay in Neutral Zone? How do you know?
- Did Fogging work? Why?

3 Rehearsing the Fogging technique.
   - Select a confident student to role-play with you Story 1. The teacher plays the role of Sue (the target) and the student, as Julie, plays the bully (reading the script). This gives the class the opportunity to see the strategy of Fogging in action.
   - This story is then role-played by the entire class. The teacher now plays the role of the bully (Julie) and the class responds as the target (Sue), speaking as one voice (ensuring that no one student will be labelled as a target). Observe your students, reminding them to stay in Neutral Zone and use their safety shield. Praise and encourage students so they successfully embody Fogging.
   - Invite students to give feedback on the experience, sharing fears and concerns they might have about using this strategy. Also ask them to describe some situations where Fogging would be appropriate.

4 Explain to students the meaning of Robot Voice.
   (Robot Voice means repeating the same statement again and again with the same words, tone and body language. When we use Robot Voice we do not give the reaction that is expected because we stay in Neutral Zone.)

5 Read Story 2: James and Bill to the class. Ask students:
   - How would you describe Bill's body language?
   - How might Bill be feeling?
   - Did Bill stay in Neutral Zone? Why?
   - Did Robot Voice work for Bill? Why?

6 Rehearse the Robot Voice technique, as for Fogging (activity 3).

Kids at work

Students complete Activity Sheet 17. They may wish to refer to Posters 2, 3, 4 and 5 when answering some of the questions.

Coaching tip

Please use your discretion and rename the characters in the role-plays if you have students in your class with those names.

Just for fun

With your students write suitable script cards that can be used for further rehearsals of Robot Voice and Fogging.

Stories illustrating Fogging and Robot Voice

Story 1 Sue and Julie (Fogging)

It is half past three in the afternoon and Sue and Julie are in the corridor, collecting their school bags. Julie says to Sue, 'You look silly with that new haircut'.

Sue just says 'Maybe' in a cool, calm voice as she imagines her safety shield over her, bouncing the mean words back to where they came from.

'That haircut is so uncool, it went out years ago,' says Julie in a nasty voice.

'Could have,' says Sue laughing slightly as she looks Julie in the eye.

'I bet nobody likes it,' sniggers Julie.

'Possibly,' Sue replies in a casual voice.

'We're not letting you hang out with us looking like that,' Julie says, poking a mean face.

Sue shrugs her shoulders saying 'So', and continues to pack her bag.

Story 2 James and Bill (Robot Voice)

James and Bill are on school camp and Bill has brought along his camera to take photos of his friends having fun. James stamps up to Bill and says loudly, 'Give me your camera'.

Bill feels his tummy rumble and start to knot; he remembers to use his safety shield and answers in a calm, clear way, 'No, I don't lend my camera' as he puts the camera in his jacket pocket.

James yells back at Bill saying, 'Give me your camera, I won't wreck it'.

Bill looks James in the eye, standing still and says, 'No, I don't lend my camera'.

James argues back saying, 'Give me your camera or else'.

Bill stands tall and calm and says in the same tone, 'No, I don't lend my camera' as he walks over to join a group. Bill feels pleased with himself for staying in Neutral Zone and not hanging around for the situation to become worse.

Strategies for Assertiveness

Fill in Susie's responses using Fogging and Peter's response using Robot Voice.

FOGGING

Susie uses her Safety Shield and stays in Neutral Zone.

Fill in Susie's responses.

Julie: You look silly with that new haircut.

Susie: ....

Julie: That haircut is so uncool, it went out years ago.

Susie: ....

Julie: I bet nobody likes it.

Susie: ....

Julie: You're not hanging out with us looking like that.

Susie: ....

Fogging Responses

·COULD BE   ·Maybe

·SO   ·POSSIBLY   *you were so interested*

·Didn't know   ·That's what you think

Remember to repeat the same statement.

ROBOT VOICE

Peter uses his Safety Shield and stays in Neutral Zone.

Fill in Peter's responses.

Jim: Give me your camera.
Peter: No, I don't lend my camera.

Jim: Give me your camera, it's no big deal.
Peter: ....

Jim: Come on, I lent you my stuff last week.
Peter: ....

Jim: You'll be sorry if you don't lend me your camera.
Peter: ....

Illustrate either story on the back of this sheet.

Form a team. Illustrate and write your own script for Fogging and Robot Voice.

Present this to your class. Watch your body language.

 Bullying: A Whole-school Approach, ACER Press, © Copyright 2001 Amelia Suckling and Carla Temple

Self-talk – My Winning Voice

Fact file

'If our inner speech can be regarded as self-guiding, then it is also clear that the context of this inner speech can be adaptive or maladaptive' (Wragg, 1989, p. 11). It is our inner speech (self-talk) that determines and guides our behaviour. Teachers play a dynamic role in assisting students to develop self-talk that is relevant and purposeful. When students are aware of their self-talk it enables them to change the quality of their thinking, which will influence their behaviour. A student's self-talk can feed the negative belief that he or she is a vulnerable victim, a powerless bystander or a bully that needs to use power and manipulation to get what is wanted. If self-talk, is guided in a positive way it can empower a student to effectively handle challenging and confrontational behaviour.

When conducting our workshops, students share some of their self-talk statements with us. Here are some common negative self-talk statements students use: I can't; why should I?; they make me; it's not my fault; I never...; I won't...; it's not fair when they... .

We share with students that they can become their own best coach by training their brain to barrack for themselves and to make their thoughts their friends. Through structured and guided activities we invite students to listen to the quality of their self-talk and help them to realise they can choose to change this. For example: I can; I'll give it a go; it's okay to...; I can handle it when...; I'm getting better at...; tomorrow is a new day; if I don't get it right the first time I'll give it another go.

Daily life is filled with both positive and negative emotions and by encouraging and teaching our children to think about *how* they are thinking, we help them to avoid being trapped in a negative downward spiral where they may constantly tell themselves that they can't, won't or that it is someone else's fault.

To help students make distinctions between negative and positive self-talk we speak of the Losing Voice and the Winning Voice. These terms came from the students themselves when we trialled this strategy in primary schools. Students come to understand that their Winning Voice encourages them to have a go and the Losing Voice leaves them feeling defeated and put down.

Our job as teachers is to provide our students with the skills to make a conscious choice to use self-talk that will lift and enhance rather than limit and put down. This in turn will have repercussions on their school environment and in the long-term will help build an anti-bullying ethos throughout the school.

To keep students motivated and aware of their thoughts, choices and actions, we have devised the 'Safe School Service Certificate' (Appendices, page 160). It is to be given to students as appropriate and acknowledges and affirms behaviour that is inclusive, supportive and empathic.

Purpose of lesson

To introduce students to the nature of self-talk and how it affects behaviour: that it can be self-defeating or self-serving.

Learning outcome

Students investigate their internal dialogue.

Materials required

Activity Sheet 18 (page 133) for each student
Posters 6 and 7 (pages 156–7), enlarged
CD player
music
balloons (one for every two students)
butcher paper
felt pen

Activities

1 Ask students what they think is 'self-talk'. (The words that go on inside my head. Sometimes it makes me feel like a winner, sometimes it makes me feel like a loser. Each of us has a Winning Voice and a Losing Voice.) Display and refer to Posters 6 and 7 to assist class discussion.

2 Students to form pairs. Provide each pair with an inflated balloon that has a self-talk statement written on it (each balloon has a different statement). Have a mixture of positive and negative statements. Play some taped music while students flick the balloons up into the air and then tap whichever balloon floats their way. When the music stops, students hold the balloon still. Then ask two or three students to read the statement on their balloon; the class determines if the statement is positive or negative.
   • Repeat this several times.
   • List the self-talk statements that were on the balloons on the board and ask the students to categorise them into positive or negative. Pop the balloons with negative statements and throw them into the bin symbolising that *if you put garbage in, you get garbage out*. Review with the students the self-talk statements listed, changing the negative into positive statements.

3 Invite students to listen to their inner dialogue when they are told the following statements:
   • You have a maths test after lunch.
   • You are not on the team.
   • Well done, your project was excellent.
   • You're invited to the party.

4 Share responses to the above. List these on the board or on butcher paper and categorise into Winning Voice or Losing Voice. Likely responses could be:

- I hate maths.
- I'm bad at maths.
- Great, I'm pretty good at maths.
- Not another test.
- I never get picked.
- It's not fair.
- I'll give it another go.
- I'm proud of myself.
- I love going to parties.
- Why should I go to the party. I don't really know anyone.

5 Role-play the different types of body language that match the following self-talk statements:

When my Losing Voice says:

- Everyone hates me at this school.
- I hate being different
- Those kids always tease me.
- Why should I bother, it's no use.
- I never have any friends.

When my Winning Voice says:

- Not everyone has to like me.
- It's okay being me.
- I can play with someone else.
- I'll see if that kid is okay.
- I'm okay, I can join in and take turns.

6 Read the story of Jimmy Jetson that follows. Ask students to listen carefully to his self-talk.

Does he listen to his Winning Voice or his Losing Voice? Is he barracking for himself on the inside?

Jimmy Jetson story

Jimmy Jetson wakes up every morning saying to himself, *I hate school, I never have anyone to play with.* He feels a knot in his tummy as he arrives at the school. He hears himself saying, *I don't want to walk down the corridor, I bet they'll start teasing me and making rude signs behind my back.* He walks slowly towards his classroom thinking to himself, *I hate being different, I never have any friends.* As he puts his books on his desk he hears himself say, *Everyone hates me at this school, it's not fair.* He sits at his desk, feeling lonely and disinterested in school.

7 List Jimmy's self-talk statements. Replace these with positive self-talk statements.

Kids at work

Students complete Activity Sheet 18.

Coaching tips

- Encourage students to write statements in the present tense, using their Winning Voice.
- When a problem arises, whether it be related to academic or friendship issues, ask the students to check in with their self-talk. Guide them to use their Winning Voice and barrack for themselves.
- Encourage students to avoid statements using the word *try*. Example: *I'll try to get good at maths*, or *I'll try to get better.* The brain associates *try* with *being difficult.*

Just for fun

- You may wish to invite your students to write a statement on a small piece of card, using their Winning Voice. They can place it inside their folder or stick it onto their desk, wherever it will be viewed by them daily, reminding them that their thoughts influence their behaviour. So, what are they thinking?!
- Ask students to make statements about the following, using their Winning Voice:
  a a subject area that is difficult.   *My reading is getting better and better.*
  b taking on a challenge.   *I'll have a go.*
  c friendship issues.   *I'm okay, I can handle it.*
  d behavioural issues.   *I can handle myself.*
- *Creating a collage: What Am I Thinking?* Students select from magazines a variety of people with positive facial expressions and body language to cut and paste on a large sheet of paper/broadsheet. Students add thinking bubbles to each, writing in a positive self-talk statement to match.

I Listen to My Winning Voice

Sometimes my self-talk says:

my Winning Voice

Read these Winning Thoughts. Copy any
3 into the spaces provided above.

I'm getting stronger on the inside.

I can handle bullying.

I feel ok about myself.

I can ask an adult for help.

Write down what your Winning Voice
would say if you were being bullied.

I barrack for myself!

Bullying: A Whole-school Approach, ACER Press, © Copyright 2001 Amelia Suckling and Carla Temple

Using relaxation and creative visualisation

The experience of stress is a very real consequence for students who are targeted and for students who engage in bullying behaviour because both are unable to self-regulate. Some students may fall into a victim cycle where their behaviours are that of helplessness and hopelessness while others may be in a downward spiral of aggression and manipulation as the only means available to them to get what they want. Some students may be trapped in both cycles of behaviour, that of bully and of victim. Relaxation and creative visualisation are valuable life skills that not only benefit students experiencing difficulty with their peers but all students.

For those students who overreact aggressively, whether they are caught up in a victim and/or bullying cycle, relaxation can diffuse the anger and agitation, clear the mind and assist the student in regaining a sense of control. For those students who overreact with tears, sulking, whingeing and helplessly giving in to threats, relaxation and creative visualisation can calm the emotions, reduce anxiety and clear out negative thoughts. By creating an improved sense of well-being, confidence increases to handle issues of conflict. Spivach and Shure state that for 'students who do not possess the prerequisites of self-control, an intermediary programme of relaxation may be necessary to slow children down to a level where they can premeditate and predetermine their behaviour' (cited in Besag, 1989, p. 34).

Regular practice of relaxation and creative visualisation sends a positive message to the school community. The practice equips students with the skills to:

- build personal well-being
- develop self-control
- develop self-reliance.

We believe that personal enquiry assists in building inner strength and is the most worthwhile gift to give the young to navigate their future.

In this lesson we want to share our experience and the benefits of teaching relaxation and creative visualisation to students in primary schools. But first, we need to define some terms.

Relaxation is a process of letting go of tension, anger and tiredness that builds and stores in one's body and mind. This is done through relaxing the body muscles, focused breathing and creative visualisation.

Creative visualisation is the process of directing the imagination to bring about positive change in one's life. It can be used to set goals, assist decision making, increase self-awareness and improve the quality of one's life.

Channel Perfect Positive Screen (Channel PPS)   We explain to young students that inside their minds they have their very own television screen that is portable and private. Just like with a television, they can change the channel in order to change what they see. In fact, changing their thoughts is as quick as changing the channel on television. They choose the pictures on their screen, pictures of who they are and what they want to be.

We decided, with feedback from the students, to name this strategy Channel Perfect Positive Screen (PPS). This name helps students to understand that their thoughts are visual images in their mind that influence their choices and ultimately their behaviour. Students in our workshops talk of using Channel Perfect Positive Screen as a means of seeing themselves getting better at school work, sport, making friends and fixing up problems.

Purpose of lesson

To give students the experience of physical relaxation and for them to creatively visualise by switching on to their Channel Perfect Positive Screen.

Learning outcomes

- Students experience relaxation and creative visualisation as tools for emptying out negative feelings and replacing these with positive feelings.
- Students visualise successful outcomes on their Channel Perfect Positive Screen.

Materials required

Activity Sheet 19 (page 140) for each student
Posters 6 and 7 (Appendices, pages 156–7), enlarged
portable CD player
classroom suitably arranged for relaxation (see activities, 4)
relaxation script (pages 138–9)
personal selection of music to accompany script
butcher paper
felt pens

Activities

1 Ask and discuss with students the following questions:
   - How many thoughts do we have a day? (thousands)
   - Where do our thoughts come from? (our mind/brain)
   - How well do we treat this organ in our body?
   - What do we do if we want to improve at swimming or athletics? (train, work our muscles)
   - How do we train our brain/mind? (making positive pictures about ourself on the television screen in our mind – rehearsing success, training the brain to create pictures that barrack for ourselves)
   - Who is the boss of your brain and your thinking?

- When pictures come up on your television at home and you don't like it, what do you do? (use remote control to change it)
- Do you think you can do the same with the pictures you see on your own television screen in your mind?
- Who would like to have their own success channel on the television screen in their mind? (introduce Channel Perfect Positive Screen – Channel PPS)

2 Ask students to close their eyes and visualise these scenes on their Channel PPS:
  - having a fight with a friend; replace this with making up
  - being alone; replace this with joining a new group
  - feeling teased and put down; replace this with standing firm in Neutral Zone
  - looking shy with weak body language; replace this with looking confident.

3 Display Posters 6 and 7 to illustrate to the students how our thoughts influence the images we make and the words we hear inside our mind. We choose whether these are self-defeating or self-serving.

4 Guide students through the relaxation and creative visualisation experience as outlined below. You may choose to use the script on pages 138–9.

Preparing for relaxation in the classroom

Having your classroom and resources ready in advance to create a conducive mood contributes to a successful session.

- Place a note on your door that reads, *Relaxation in progress; please return in 15 minutes.*
- Ask students to remove shoes (optional).
- Close the blinds and turn off lights.
- If necessary, ask specific children to lie in specially allocated places to minimise distractions.
- For some children closing their eyes for any reason other than sleep is difficult. Ask all students to bring a soft scarf to school which they can gently place over their eyes during the relaxation. Practise and model how eyes need to be closed.
- Model to children the correct way to lie on the floor (flat on your back with arms and legs uncrossed, arms gently by your sides with palms facing up).
- To avoid children dramatically huffing and puffing, it is important to explain to them to breathe gently through their nose so that they do not disturb others.
- If reading the script, keep your voice calm, clear and quiet.
- Remind children that this time is just for them.

Completion of the relaxation session

- At the completion of each session bring students back to the reality of the classroom slowly. This can be done by asking children to focus on the sounds they can hear in their environment and becoming aware of their physical body by gently wriggling their fingers and toes. Let the students sit up in their own time.
- Allow time for students to reflect and share their relaxation experience.

5 Ask students about their experience of the relaxation session. How did it feel? Did they enjoy it? experience anything in particular?

Divide the class into manageable-sized groups and ask each group to write their responses on butcher paper to share with the class.

6 Discuss with students at what times they could imagine using their Channel Perfect Positive Screen. A sample of student responses might include: when I feel angry; when I've had a fight with a friend or mum and dad; when I'm upset; when my head feels full; when I feel worried; when I can't get to sleep; when I don't feel well.

7 Ask students what it's like for them to experience the feeling of relaxation. In what ways is it good for them? (Often what comes up in our sessions is that relaxation is practised to rest and re-energise the body, calm and empty the mind and reduce anxiety.)

Kids at work

Students complete Activity Sheet 19.

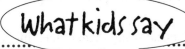

Students provide us with astute comments on their experiences and feelings. Here are some responses that have come out of our workshops in primary schools.

Relaxation feels:

- like I'm floating
- like I'm melting
- like I can forget about my life
- like I can empty out my head.

Channel Perfect Positive Screen

- I use it when I feel tense and hopeless and to make good things happen.
- I enjoy the Channel PPS the best because it gives me a new way of facing my problems.
- When I am sad I can go to Channel PPS and it makes me happy. And I am glad we do it because it helps everyone's feelings.

Relaxation script

This time of relaxation is just for you. Nobody else is important right now, just you. It is time for you to empty out and re-energise your mind, to make it healthy and strong on the inside.

Your mind is the powerhouse to your body and thoughts, so feed it with the best food you can and that's positive thinking.

Now you have found a quiet place to enjoy relaxation, make yourself warm and comfortable; make sure your spine is straight. All you need do is just breathe and listen, and remember this special time is just for you.

Let's begin by breathing deeply and quietly: through your nose and out through your mouth and in through your nose and out through your mouth. Keep breathing, letting go as you breathe out, remembering this special time is just for you.

Now let your feet feel soft, loose and relaxed, allowing them to feel warm and tingly. Let this feeling travel up your legs, allowing both legs to feel warm, soft and relaxed.

Now let your tummy feel warm and empty like a lovely melting feeling deep inside, making you feel more and more relaxed. This feeling travels up to your chest. Every breath you take you sink deeper and deeper into relaxation, allowing this tingling feeling to make you feel warm and safe.

Let's go even further as you now relax your shoulders, allowing them to melt into a comfortable position and tingle with relaxation. Now let your mouth, eyes, nose and forehead go, feeling loose and relaxed, allowing your face to feel soothed and gentle.

This feeling now travels down both arms to the tips of your fingers, making them feel soft, warm and relaxed. It's truly safe and wonderful to let go, allowing this warm feeling to spread over your entire body. Relaxation is good for your body and good for your mind.

Now that your body is fully relaxed, you are ready to see the TV screen in your mind. Switch on to Channel Perfect Positive Screen. Your Channel PPS. Your screen is clear, colourful and ready just for you to make all the wonderful pictures you wish.

You see a large, colourful hot-air balloon with a basket underneath. You place into the

Coaching tip

Remind students that practising new or challenging behaviour on their Channel Perfect Positive Screen first can make it easier to bring about required changes and to carry out their plans successfully.

Just for fun

- To illustrate the impact that relaxation has, you can fill a small plastic bag with soft, dry sand then cut one corner. The slow but steady emptying out of the sand is an easy and visual metaphor to use with students.

hot-air balloon all your negative feelings. You may be feeling sad, angry or worried about something. Put all these feelings into the basket of the hot-air balloon. That's right, let all those feelings go. Maybe you're feeling lighter now. Isn't it great to let go? The hot air balloon gently floats away, higher and higher into the clear blue sky until you can no longer see it. You feel better and better.

A new and happy picture appears on your Channel Perfect Positive Screen. See the bright, colourful picture of yourself. You're smiling and feeling confident about who you are. Each day you feel stronger and stronger on the inside. You understand that feeling strong on the inside starts with your thoughts.

Every day is a new opportunity to let yourself shine:

to barrack for yourself with your thoughts

to stay in Neutral Zone when you want to react to the actions and words of others

to build happy and new friendships.

Listen to your Winning Voice inside your mind. It is saying, *I'll give it a go. I'm in control of myself, it's okay to be different.*

You make a picture of yourself standing firm in Neutral Zone, feeling in control of yourself, barracking for yourself with your thoughts. You stand tall, and your voice is clear and calm. You like what you see. You see yourself as part of a happy friendship group, taking turns, encouraging your friends and having fun. Take time now to enjoy that feeling and the picture you see of yourself.

You invite a party of happy thoughts to join you.

You make those thoughts your friends. Those thoughts make you feel great.

Switch off your Channel Perfect Positive Screen, knowing you can return there any time and many times each day.

Now let your body gently stretch, bringing your hands up over your head. If you are lying down, bring your knees up to your chest. And when you are ready, sit up slowly and gently, ready to greet the rest of your day.

- You may wish to make relaxation a daily classroom practice. Straight after lunch is often a troublesome time for teachers resolving playground disputes. A 10–15-minute relaxation exercise can help diffuse any negative emotions that may be brought back to the classroom and put possible issues into better perspective.

    Use relaxation after sport when students may feel tired and need re-energising.
- Students can apply Channel PPS to a variety of situations: visualising their personal best in sport; visualising improved academic performance and task completion; visualising trying something new; visualising making new friends.

I Switch On to Channel Perfect Positive Screen

In each of the above TV screens draw yourself:

1 handling a bullying situation.
2 joining a group of friends.
3 standing firm in Neutral Zone.

Write down examples of the times you can switch on to Channel PPS:

- making up with friends

- ....

- ....

- ....

   Bullying: A Whole-school Approach, ACER Press, © Copyright 2001 Amelia Suckling and Carla Temple

APPENDICES

Related literature for students

Picture books

Browne, Anthony. *Willy the Wimp*. Walker Books, London, 1984.
—— *Willy and Hugh*. Walker Books, London, 1991.
—— *Willy the Champ*. Walker Books, London, 1993.
—— *Willy the Dreamer*. Walker Books, London, 1997.
Hughes, David. *Bully*. Walker Books, London, 1995.
Morimoto, Junko. *The Two Bullies*. Random House, Sydney, 1997.
Stanley, Elizabeth. *Deliverance of Dancing Bears*. Puffin, Ringwood VIC, 1995.
Velthuijs, Mac. *Frog and the Stranger*. Anderson Press, London, 1993.

Lower–middle primary

Fine, Anne. *Angel of Nitshill Road*. Mammoth, London, 1993.
Gleeson, Libby. *Skating on Sand*. Viking, Ringwood VIC, 1994.
—— *Hannah Plus One*. Puffin, Ringwood VIC, 1996.
Orr, Wendy. *Bully Biscuit Gang*. Angus & Robertson, Sydney, 1998.
Sefton, Catherine. *Watch Out, Fred's About*. Hamish Hamilton, London, 1996.
Slater, Teddy. *Who's Afraid of Big Bad Bully*. Scholastic, New York, 1995.

Middle–upper primary

Blume, Judy. *Blubber*. Macmillan, London, 1988.
Caswell, Brian. *Mike*. University of Queensland Press, Brisbane, 1993.
Chambers, Aidan. *The Present Takers*. Bodley Head, London, 1983.
Curtis, C.P. *Watsons Go to Birmingham*. Random House, New York, 1992.
Forrestal, Elaine. *Someone Like Me*. Puffin, Ringwood VIC, 1996.
Gervay, Susanne. *I Am Jack*. Angus & Robertson, Sydney, 2000.
Gowar, Mick. *Jimmy Woods and the Big Bad Wolf*. A&C Black, London, 1994.
Henry, Maeve. *Listen to the Dark*. Heinemann, London, 1993.
Hilton, Nette. *The Hiccup*. Angus & Robertson, Sydney, 1992.
McKay, Amanda. *Sally Marshall's Not An Alien*. University of Queensland Press, Brisbane, 1994.
Needle, Jan. *The Bully*. Hamish Hamilton, London, 1993.
Scott, Hugh. *The Camera Obscura*. Walker Books, London, 1990.
Thiele, Colin. *Danny's Egg*. Angus & Robertson, Sydney, 1989.

Upper primary–lower secondary

Byars, Betsy. *The Eighteenth Emergency*. Random House, London, 1994.
Carmody, Isobel. *The Gathering*. Puffin, Ringwood VIC, 1993.
Cormier, Robert. *The Chocolate War*. Collins, London, 1974.
Gee, Maurice. *The Fat Man*. Viking, Auckland, 1994.
Gleeson, Libby. *Dodger*. Penguin, Ringwood VIC, 1992.
Hawthorn, Libby. *Thunderwith*. Heinemann, Melbourne, 1989.

Hill, David. *Fat, Four-Eyed and Useless*. Scholastic, Auckland, 1997.

Klein, Robin. *All in the Blue Unclouded Weather*. Viking, Ringwood VIC, 1991.

Lindquist, Rowena Cory. *Capped*. Scholastic, Sydney, 1996.

MacFarlane, Peter. *Bruce the Goose*. Angus & Robertson, Sydney, 1997.

Provoost, Anne. *Falling*. Allen & Unwin, Sydney, 1997.

Stewart, Maureen. *Easy Meat*. Random House, Sydney, 1997.

Wild, Margaret. *Beast*. Omnibus, Adelaide, 1992.

We would like to acknowledge the work of Christine Andell from The Little Bookroom (Victoria, Australia) and Linning, Phillips and Turton, authors of *A Literature-based Approach to Bullying* (1997).

(photocopy onto school letterhead)

Dear Parent/Guardian,

Did you know that Australian studies show that one in five students are continually bullied and that many students are reluctant to report a bullying incident? Our school is taking positive action to create a safe and happy environment for all our students.

Our class is currently working on a unit of work about anti-bullying, which covers topics such as:

- what is bullying?
- how it feels to be bullied
- why kids bully
- locating bullying in our school
- actions the bystander can take
- the importance of responsible reporting
- strategies for assertiveness
- handling bullying behaviour
- whole-school strategies.

I encourage your child to share with you what he/she has learnt at school. Thank you for your support as we continue to build a safe and happy school.

Yours sincerely,

(photocopy onto school letterhead)

Dear Parent/Guardian,

Our school is continuing to take pro-active steps in building a safe and supportive learning environment. We are currently addressing the issue of anti-bullying. Our role is to continue to raise awareness within the school community and adopt best practice.

We will be seeking input from the students by conducting anonymous surveys. These will help in the planning, updating and implementation of effective prevention and intervention strategies and in the evaluation of our current practices.

We encourage students to talk with their families about this issue. We appreciate your support and will keep you informed.

Yours sincerely,

Bullying: A Whole-school Approach, ACER Press, © Copyright 2001 Amelia Suckling and Carla Temple

Monitoring Negative Behaviours

NAME: .... DATE: ....

CLASS TEACHER: .... YEAR LEVEL: ....

Motives for Misbehaviour: *Power, Revenge, Attention-seeking, Withdrawal*

THE BEHAVIOURS	WHERE THEY OCCUR	WHEN THEY OCCUR	PEER REACTION

Bullying: A Whole-school Approach, ACER Press, © Copyright 2001 Amelia Suckling and Carla Temple

I Barrack for Myself

The behaviour I am working on is:...
....
....

I won't:

....
....
....
....

I will:

....
....
....
....

BAD STUFF: *(With student, list 2 or 3 consequences of not adopting appropriate behaviour.)*

....
....
....

GOOD STUFF: *(With student, list 2 or 3 consequences of adopting appropriate behaviour.)*

....
....
....

I coach myself when I choose to:

....
....
....
....

(With student, list 3 or 4 safe behaviours he or she can do when feeling negative.)

My teacher coaches me by:

....
....
....
....
....

Consequences of not following my plan:...
....
....

SIGNATURES: ....

DATE TO START: ....   REVIEW DATE: ....

My Record of Behaviour

NAME: ....

YEAR LEVEL: .... DATE: ....

MONDAY	TUESDAY	WEDNESDAY	THURSDAY	FRIDAY

Coaching tips from my teacher

😊😊😊 I'm doing well

😊😊 I'm doing okay

☹ I'm not doing so well

My rewards

....

....

....

Tips for teachers of students who bully

Make it clear to the student that the school community takes the issue of bullying seriously and that it is unacceptable behaviour. Give support in a variety of ways, through providing a mentor, supervision and programs.

Think about *why* the student is bullying. Could it be the result of any or all of the following:

1 Boredom

Brainstorm with student suitable activities to do at lunchtime.

2 Frustration

Investigate if the work load is too difficult or too easy.
Investigate if the student has a peer group to which he or she belongs.

3 Anger

Is the student angry? Share with the student that anger is a normal human emotion; it is what we do with the anger that makes it constructive or destructive. Provide strategies to diffuse the anger within the framework of these precepts:
- You must not hurt yourself.
- You must not hurt others.
- You must not hurt property.
Together devise a menu of appropriate anger diffusers that fit the above criteria.

4 Lack of social skills

Some students may have difficulty making distinctions between aggressive and assertive behaviour. You may wish to play back to students some of the ways they are behaving that are ineffective and then model to them ways of getting what they want without having to be manipulative or aggressive. Always seek permission from the students first to role-play their existing behaviour back to them.

5 Low empathy

With a sensitive and non-judgmental approach, help the student to understand the effects of his or her behaviour on others. Explore the problem with the student and encourage him or her to develop empathy by asking questions such as: When you treat X in that way, how do you think X feels? Is there another way you could do this?

At all times avoid aggressive verbal tactics; this only reinforces the type of behaviour you are wanting to counter in the student.

Checklist for signs of bullying

Many students are reluctant to report bullying for fear of reprisal, shame, humiliation, feelings of inadequacy and a belief that telling someone will not improve the situation.

Teachers need to be constantly on the lookout for signs that may indicate bullying is going on. The points listed below provide some clues that students may be being bullied; they may also indicate other issues. Further enquiry may be necessary to establish the real cause.

Physical signs

- ☐ Cuts and bruises
- ☐ Money lost
- ☐ Damage to property
- ☐ Torn clothing

Psychological signs

- ☐ Mood swings
- ☐ Uncharacteristically quiet
- ☐ Less approachable
- ☐ Nightmares
- ☐ Non-specific pain
- ☐ Destructive or self-destructive behaviour
- ☐ Bouts of apathy and depression
- ☐ Difficult to manage
- ☐ Over-sensitive
- ☐ Weepy

Social signs

- ☐ Doesn't seem to have any friends
- ☐ Putting in less effort and doing less at school
- ☐ Giving up on hobbies
- ☐ Reluctance about coming to school
- ☐ Secretive
- ☐ Missing personal belongings

Bullying: A Whole-school Approach, ACER Press, © Copyright 2001 Amelia Suckling and Carla Temple

My Winning Voice

Congratulations

....

is awarded the

Beaut Bystander Certificate

Congratulations, your positive actions make a difference to our school.

Teacher: .... Date: ....

Congratulations

....

is awarded the

Great Mate Certificate

Congratulations for including and encouraging your classmates.

Teacher: .... Date: ....

Congratulations

....

is awarded the

Safe School Service Certificate

Congratulations for helping to make the school a safe and happy place.

We are proud of you.

Teacher: .... *Date:* ....

Bibliography

Books and journal articles

Argyle, M. (1983). *The Psychology of Interpersonal Relationships* (4th ed.). Harmondsworth: Penguin.

Back, K. and Back, K. (1991). *Assertiveness at Work*. London: McGraw Hill.

Berne, S. (1996). *Bully-Proof Your Child*. Melbourne: Lothian.

Besag, V. (1989). *Bullies and Victims in Schools*. Philadelphia: Open University Press.

Besag, V. (1992). *We Don't Have Bullies Here*. 57 Manor House Rd, Newcastle-upon-Tyne.

Biddulph, S. (1997). *Raising Boys*. Sydney: Finch Publishing.

Boulton, M.J. and Underwood, K. (1992). Bully/victim problems among middle school children. *British Journal of Educational Psychology*, 73-87.

Brown, J. and Farby, L. (1993). *Overcoming Bullying – The Chalkface Project*. P.O. Box 1, Milton Keynes MK5 6JB.

Canter, L. (1992). *Assertive Discipline*. Santa Monica: Lee Canter & Associates.

Day, J. (1994). *Creative Visualization with Children*. Shaftesbury, Dorset: Element Books.

Education Department of Queensland (1998). *Bullying – No Way!*. Brisbane.

Elliot, M. (ed.) (1992). *Bullying: A Practical Guide to Coping for Schools*. London: Longman.

Elliot, M. (1998). *Wise Guides, Bullying*. London: Hodder Children's Books.

Farrington, D.P. (1993). Understanding and preventing bullying. In Tonny, M. and Morris, N. (eds), *Crime and Justice*, 17. Chicago: University of Chicago Press.

Felner, R.D. and Adan. A.A. (1988). The school transitional environment project: An ecological intervention and evaluation. In R.H. Price, E.L. Cowen *et al.* (eds), *Fourteen Ounces of Prevention*, 111-22. Washington: American Psychological Association.

Field, E.M. (1999). *Bully Busting*. Sydney: Finch Publishing.

Forsey, C. (1994). *Hands Off! The Anti-Violence Guide to Developing Positive Relationships*. Melbourne: West Education Centre, DEET.

Fuller, A. (1998). *From Surviving to Thriving: Promoting Mental Health in Young People*. Melbourne: Australian Council for Educational Research.

Gilmartin, B.G. (1987). Peer group antecedents of severe love-shyness in males. *Journal of Personality*, 55, 467-89.

Glasser, W. (1969). *Schools Without Failure*. New York: Harper & Row.

Gordon, T. (1988). *Parent Effectiveness Training*. Solana Beach, California: Effectiveness Training.

Hazler, R.J., Hoover, J.H. and Oliver, R. (1993). What do kids say about bullying? *Education Digest*, 58 (7), 16-20.

Herron, R., and Peter, V.J. (1998). *A Good Friend: How To Make One, How To Be One*. Nebraska: Boystown Press.

Hill, S. (1992). *Games That Work*. Melbourne: Eleanor Curtain Publishing.

Jenkin, J. (1996). *Resolving Violence*. Melbourne: Australian Council for Educational Research.

Johns, B.H. and Carr, V.G. (1995). *Techniques for Managing Verbally and Physically Aggressive Students.* Denver: Love Publishing.

Johnson, D.W. and Johnson, F. (1994). *Joining Together: Group Theory and Group Skills* (5th ed.). Boston: Allyn & Bacon.

Kids Helpline (1996). *School Counselling – A client-centred perspective,* August. Brisbane: Kids Helpline.

Linning, L., Phillips, M. and Turton, R. (1997). *A Literature-based Approach to Bullying.* Brisbane: The Literature Base Publications.

Marano, H.E. (1995). Big bad bully. *Psychology Today,* September/October, 58-82.

McCarthy, P., Sheehan, M., Wilkie, S., and Wilkie, W. (eds) (1998). *Bullying: Causes, Costs and Cure.* P.O. Box 196, Nathan, Queensland: Beyond Bullying Association.

Mellor, A. (1993). *Bullying and How To Fight It.* Glasgow: Scottish Council for Research in Education.

Olweus, D. (1993). *Bullying at School: What We Know and What We Can Do.* Oxford: Blackwell.

Oskamp, S. (1984). *Applied Social Psychology.* Ingelwood Cliffs, New Jersey: Prentice-Hall.

Pearson, M. and Nolan, P. (1991). *Emotional First Aid for Children.* Springwood, New South Wales: Butterfly Books.

Pearson, M. and Nolan, P. (1995). *Emotional Release for Children.* Melbourne: Australian Council for Educational Research.

Randall, P. (1996). *A Community Approach to Bullying.* London: Trentham Books.

Rigby, K. (1994). School Bullies. *Independent Teacher,* 10 (2), 8-9.

Rigby, K. (1995). New thinking about bullying in schools. *Independent Education,* July, 3-6. Sydney: New South Wales Education Union.

Rigby, K. (1996). *Bullying In Schools and What To Do About It.* Melbourne: Australian Council For Educational Research.

Rigby, K. (1997). What children tell us about bullying in schools. *Children Australia,* 22 (2), 28-34.

Rigby, K. (1998). Peer relations at school and the health of adolescents. *Youth Australia Studies,* 17 (1), 13-17.

Rigby, K. (2001). *Stop the Bullying: A Handbook for Schools.* Melbourne: Australian Council for Educational Research.

Rogers, B. (1994). *Behaviour Recovery.* Melbourne: Australian Council for Educational Research.

Rogers, B. (1998). *You Know the Fair Rule.* Melbourne: Australian Council for Educational Research.

Seligman, M. (1991). *Learned Optimism.* Sydney: Random House.

Sharp, S. and Smith, P.(eds) (1994a). *Tackling Bullying in Your School.* London: Routledge.

Sharp, S. and Smith, P. (eds) (1994b). *School Bullying.* London: Routledge.

Slee, P.T. (1995). Peer victimisation and its relationship to depression among Australian primary school students. *Personality and Individual Differences,* 18, 57-62.

Slee, P.T. (1996). *The P.E.A.C.E. Pack.* Adelaide: School of Education, Flinders University.

Smith, P. and Thompson D. (eds) (1991). *Practical Approaches to Bullying.* London: David Fulton Publishers.

St John Brooks, C. (1985). The school bullies. *New Society,* 6 December, 262-5.

Tattum, D. and Tattum, E. (1994). Countering bullying: raising awareness and developing strategies. *Incorporated Association of Registered Teachers of Victoria,* seminar series, 37, October.

Webster-Doyle, T. (1991). *Why Is Everybody Always Picking On Me?* Middlebury, Vermont: Atrium Society Publications.

Wragg, J. (1989). *Talk Sense To Yourself.* Melbourne: Australian Council for Educational Research.

Zarzour, Kim (1994). *The Schoolyard Bully.* Toronto: Harper Collins.

Associated documents

Department of Education, Victoria (1999). *Framework for Student Support Services in Victorian Government Schools.* Melbourne.

House of Representatives Standing Committee on Employment, Education and Training (1993). *Violence in Schools.* Canberra.

Videos

Maines, B. and Robinson, G. (1992). *Michael's Story – The No Blame Approach.* Bristol: Lame Duck Publishing.

Balfour, J. (1994). *Bullying.* Melbourne: Australian Council for Educational Research.

Index